Modern Poetry in Translation
Series Three, Number 7

Love and War

Edited by David and Helen Constantine

MODERN POETRY IN TRANSLATION

Modern Poetry in Translation
Series Three, No. 7
© Modern Poetry in Translation 2007 and contributors
ISBN 978-0-9545367-7-0 (and 0-9545367-7-0

Printed and bound in Great Britain by Short Run Press, Exeter

Editors: David and Helen Constantine
Reviews Editor: Josephine Balmer
Administrators: Deborah de Kock and Angela Holton

Submissions should be sent in hard copy, with return postage, to David and Helen Constantine, *Modern Poetry in Translation*, The Queen's College, Oxford, OX1 4AW. Unless agreed in advance, submissions by email will not be accepted. Only very exceptionally will we consider work that has already been published elsewhere. Translators are themselves responsible for obtaining any necessary permissions. Since we do sometimes authorize further publication on one or two very reputable websites of work that has appeared in *MPT*, the permissions should cover that possibility.

Founding Editors: Ted Hughes and Daniel Weissbort

Subscription Rates: (including postage)

	UK	Overseas
Single Issue	£11	£13 / US$ 24
One year subscription (2 issues, surface mail)	£22	£26 / US$ 48
Two year subscription (4 issues, surface mail)	£40	£48 / US$ 88

To subscribe please use the subscription form at the back of the magazine. Discounts available.

To pay by credit card please visit www.mptmagazine.com

Modern Poetry in Translation is represented in UK by Central Books, 99 Wallis Road, London, E9 5LN

For orders: tel +44 (0) 845 458 9910 Fax +44 (0) 845 458 9912 or visit www.mptmagazine.com

Modern Poetry in Translation Limited. A Company Limited by Gurantee. Registered in England and Wales, Number 5881603.
UK Registered Charity Number 1118223.

Contents

1   Editorial

5   **Adonis**, nine poems, translated by Peter Clark and Sarah Maguire

12   **Jeff Nosbaum**, 'Pride of Ajax'

14   **Yannis Ritsos**, twenty-eight of the *Monochords*, translated by Paul Merchant

18   **Guillaume Apollinaire**, seven poems, translated by Stephen Romer

27   **Pushkin**, *The Captain's Daughter*, extracts translated by Robert Chandler

41   **Vénus Khoury-Ghata**, six poems from *Interments*, translated by Marilyn Hacker

45   *Gilgamesh*, an extract translated by Paul Batchelor

48   **Federico Garcia Lorca**, 'Song of the Civil Guard', translated by Mark Leech

54   **Oliver Reynolds**, 'Kolin' and 'Dusty Miller Breaks his Silence' (after Liliencron's 'Wer weiss wo' and 'Vergiss die Mühle nicht')

57   **Stephen Romer**, four poems

64   **Du Fu**, two poems, translated by Paul Harris

68   **Charles Dobzynski**, 'My Life as a Wall', translated by Marilyn Hacker

75   **Lucretius**, 'Aulis', translated by Stephanie Norgate

78   **Robert Desnos**, ten poems, translated by Timothy Adès

90 **Anzhelina Polonskaya**, four poems, translated by Andrew Wachtel

94 **Manuel Rivas**, six poems, translated by Jonathan Dunne

100 **Giuseppe Belli**, four sonnets, translated by Mike Stocks

107 **Elsa Morante**, *Farewell*, an extract translated by Cristina Viti

118 **Andrea Zanzotto**, four poems, translated by Jo Catling and others

128 **Elena Shvarts**, nine poems, translated by Sasha Dugdale

Reviews and Comments

138 **Michael Hamburger** on Assia Wevill

141 **Robin Fulton** on Robin Robertson's Tranströmer

147 **Sasha Dugdale** on Emily Lygo's Voltskaia

150 **Charlie Louth** on Eavan Boland and the Bachmann-Henze correspondence

154 **Belinda Cooke** on translations of Vittorio Sereni and Luciano Erba

159 **Josephine Balmer**, Shorter Reviews

164 Notes on Contributors

169 *MPT* Back Issues

Editorial

Eros and Thanatos, love and death, loving and killing, love and war, are ancient in us, and opposites. Life is a continual struggle between the two and it is not only finally but very often along the way that Thanatos wins. Some lives are lived in thrall to death and only serving death, and the physical end of such lives is only the conclusion of a serial.

Love in literature – and there must be grounds for this in real living – has from the first adopted the imagery of war to say what it feels like and to describe and further the lover's means and ends. So Sappho begs Aphrodite to be her 'σύμμαχος', her fellow-fighter, in love's war. With her aid she hopes to win. And Wyatt, after Petrarch, moves to and fro in a similar imagery: 'I find no peace, and all my war is done.' Love, like an army, camps, spreads its banner, lives or dies 'in the field'. Mostly, in literature and the life it springs from, it is the man who plans and campaigns; who makes advances; who is repulsed; who counter-attacks. It might be love they are writing about, but the language is often that of calculation and, in the end, of force. It is getting, not being. The woman, the citadel, is taken. The *Liaisons dangereuses*, written by an army man, is one long extended and literalized metaphor: love as war. The love of the two chief opponents, Merteuil and Valmont, spreads into their relations with all others, involving

them in their own mortal combat. Kleist's verse play
Penthesilea, the very thought of which gave Goethe the creeps,
radically and thoroughly stages the metaphor of love's war – on
the battlefield outside Troy, Achilles against the Amazon
queen. She wins, tearing him with her teeth, proving on his
flesh the proximity of kissing and biting. In German the words
rhyme, as she observes; and the realization, the dawning
consciousness of that closeness and that she has enacted it, kills
her, having killed him.

Would any writer still want to play with war, real war, in
the expression of love? Was Apollinaire the last? In the poems
we print here he revels exuberantly in the imagery of the
battlefield, thinking of Lou. In a poem absent here, his 'Si je
mourais là-bas', strange companion-piece for Brooke's 'If I
should die . . .', he imagines (after a shell falling and opening
like mimosa) a rain of blood further reddening the lips
and nipples of his beloved, a sort of drenching of the universe,
for a greater vitality, with the red precipitation of whole-
sale slaughter. Strange and troubling conceit, Eros against
Thanatos, erotic imagination against the ugly fact of over-
whelming and mechanical death. Would anyone still want to
write like that? After the last century's wars and the wars we
started this one with? Countries, like women, taken; and rape,
real rape, at the heart of it, and not just as excess and accident,
but as enacted policy. War was always like that. But it is
omnipresent now. Remote from the current war-zones, we
know their images. And we know to the point of nausea the
pornography of men in suits and uniforms salivating over
phallic weaponry. We know, we know. The pictures them-
selves, the official and sanctioned pornography, should be
enough to deter us from mixing love and war.

Marx thought capitalism intrinsically belligerent. Trade
wars become gunboats and invasions very naturally. Many seem
to think, after our famous victory in the Cold War, that
capitalism is the one true faith and the right and natural form
for all human dealings, endpoint and summit of humanity's

evolution. Others don't think that and hope that those who do won't always prevail. There was a man from Vodaphone on the Today programme not long ago. He was talking about the new markets just opening up to his company in India. India, he said, is only thirteen percent penetrated. He was excited, there is no other word for it. He said it again, amazed and excited: 'Only thirteen – that is ONE THREE – percent penetrated!' Europe, on the other hand, is more than a hundred percent penetrated.

Love played with the language of war; war and belligerent capitalism hijack the language of love and sex. It matters, what language you use. Metaphors get literalized very easily.

'Make Love not War' is unequivocal. Good monosyllables, easy to understand.

David and Helen Constantine
March 2007

The Next Issue of *MPT*

The autumn issue of *Modern Poetry in Translation* (Third Series, Number 8) will be called 'Getting it Across'.

We want translated and original poems, short essays, anecdotes that treat the many ways in which people (and perhaps not just people) seek to communicate with one another. Translation in a very fundamental sense: getting yourself across. We should be glad of contributions on 'signing' (the language of the deaf and dumb); on pidgin, patois and creole (languages partaking of one another, or simplifying and fusing to make dealings between them possible); and on any other strategies, their successes and their failures, in the struggle to make oneself understood.

Secret languages might come into this too, the argot of people safeguarding their own dealings and identity; and, at the far end of secrecy, the idioglossia invented by children.

Submissions should be sent by 1 August 2007, please, in hard copy, with return postage, to The Editors, *Modern Poetry in Translation*, The Queen's College, Oxford, OX1 4AW. Unless agreed in advance, submissions by e-mail will not be accepted. Only every exceptionally will we consider work that has already been published elsewhere. Translators are themselves responsible for obtaining any necessary permissions. Since we do sometimes authorize further publication on one or two very reputable websites of work that has appeared in *MPT*, the permissions should cover that possibility.

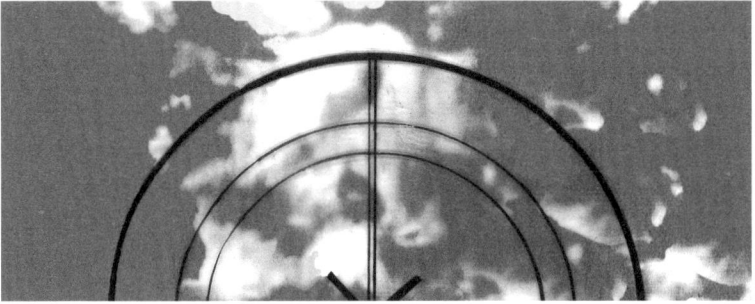

Adonis
Nine Poems
Translated by Peter Clark and Sarah Maguire

Adonis is the pen-name of Ali Ahmad Said. He was born 1930 in Syria but has spent the greater part of his life as a writer in the Lebanon. His career has been turbulent and, like so many Arab writers, he has experienced imprisonment and exile. He is one of the Arab world's leading spokesmen. As such he has (paradoxically) been a channel for European influences on Arab poetry, and at the same time a vociferous opponent of Western values. 'We no longer believe in Europe. We no longer have faith in its political system or in its philosophies.' All the same, as a francophone who now lives in Paris, his cultural heroes include Marx, Baudelaire, Apollinaire, Gramsci, Goethe and Rilke.

(Adapted from Robert Irwin in *The Oxford Guide to Contemporary Writing.*)

(1)

> As though death just   shoots straight past me –
> eyes down   biting its tongue

> As though death falls asleep   only
> when I fall asleep

(2)

> Pot basil on the windowsill   its pungent aroma
> infusing the house

> your hands   cupped
> make a balcony

> your hands   cupped
> in greeting

> Years ago now   before I had any idea
> how this house   was lit up with love

> This was years ago   before
> my solitary star   found its constellation

> before my solitary star   slipped into place
> amongst friends

> (It was even before   that time
> when my star   fell from grace
> the time   I was lost in a labyrinth of loss)

But in those far-off days   the dawn flooded my room
                            mapping my possessions
and the sun turned   my bedclothes my notebook
                            my hands
                            into fixed points on a sundial
all charting its progress   day long through the heavens

                            Look

                            the small hills break into bloom
                            the far coastline is radiant
                            cold springs tell their prayers
                                     to the grasses
even the sapling branches conduct the four winds

(3)

the square is packed out –
       every last soul in the village
has turned up for the *craic*

a dog-tired old man
       leans against a doorway
an exhausted old woman
       collapses on a bench

the session settles down
       into ardent discussion
sharp memories, sweet regrets
       circle the village

old wounds are salved
       the lit-up faces
don't notice the dark

even the sparrows join in
        swooping through the square
chattering and squabbling

as night falls, heat rises
        desire quickening
in the burning young men
        in the lips of young girls

whilst under the fig trees
        the faithful are chanting
pledging their allegiance
        to arcane mysteries

but our fields are bone-dry –
        the sweet rain
has not rained
        for so long

(4)

slaughter has slaughtered   the structure of the city:
            this stone   is the head of a boy
    this column of smoke   is the last breath of a girl

everything and everything   chants it is exiled
                               chants it is outcast
                               chants it is lost
                               in a lake full of blood

what can morning expect

                               except innards and entrails
                               stumbling through the mist?

what can morning expect

except cacophony
except carnage?

(5)

The Raid

the bird bursts into flames

and the horses and the women and the paving stones
are ripped up

crusts of bread crushed
in the fat fists of Taimur

(6)

Lament

Last rites:
Laid out for the wake:

My beloved:

your face is engraved
with the flowers of the forest

which bloom in your footsteps
and throng every threshold
you crossed

(7)

First Lesson

But now we can ask   how we first met
But now we can spell   the long road home

we can say   how the beach is deserted
how the fortress laid waste
is a footnote on the news

Now we can say   *We are done for*

(8)

The Woman's Face

I set up home in a woman's face

her face was at home   in the roiling waves
in the tug of the tides
washed up on the beach
adrift amongst sea-shells

I set up home in a woman's face

a face that   slaughtered me
a face that   adored me
a face that   drowned in the spume of my
blood
a face that   waited till madness had ceased

a lighthouse extinguished   rising through the dark

(9)

Maybe My Country

here I am   shinning up the fence round
                                     my country
                             scrambling over boulders
                             skirting barbed wire

            here I am   breaking out
                             of dropping dead
                             in my country

            here I am   homeless
                             and at home
                             in exile

            here I am   far from home
                             looking back at the country
                             that may be my country

                             one day

Jeff Nosbaum
'Pride of Ajax'

'Pride of Ajax' is not a translation or version as such, but was written shortly after reading Sophocles' *Ajax*. To use the title of the last issue of *MPT*, I would consider this poem an 'after-image' of Sophocles' play and a reflection on its portrait of the effects of pride, particularly in the context of war and its aftermath.

Pride of Ajax

      where being good
is not as good
      as being known
as great. Of such
      small gestures fashion
fashions tools, staccato
      ticks turned to

the wheel to teeth
    and cry and teeth
and die on one's own
    sword. A gift,
of sorts, from
    one taut cryer
to another. The toilsome
    noise of tempting
gestures, like a street
    of bleating taxis,
keeps the sounds of shame
    at bay, moored
though they be
    deep within the ear.
Those ships never will
    depart for home, that life
will never stray
    beyond the second
sight she gave: what
    might, and never could
have been. Sometimes
    there is no contingency
time. Sometimes it is
    already too late
and the gods have salved
    your eyes with spittle
so that kings seem
    cattle, cattle kings
and the efficacy
    of failure is
self-evident
    in the moment
failure takes you.

Yannis Ritsos
Twenty-eight of the *Monochords*
Translated by Paul Merchant

Ritsos wrote the three hundred and thirty-six *Monochords* in a single month, from August 1 to September 1, 1979, while in exile on the island of Samos during the Papadopoulos dictatorship. The last of the one-line poems reads: 'So you'll know – these monochords are my keys. Take them.'

In 1966, at his Athens publishers, Ritsos offered this advice on translating his poetry: 'My poetry does not adopt poses; I don't achieve effects through irony or sarcasm, but try always for a neutral tone. If you are translating the poems you will need the most up-to-date lexicon, the most demotic. Translate the words exactly as you see them.' He was dangerous to dictators because his short poems speak simple shared truths, and his longer poems on mythic subjects measure the narrow aims of demagogues against the span of history. His one-line monochords can be read as miniature encapsulations by a master of the art of brevity, or as keys to his whole work, his lexicon of images and ideas.

The full translation is to be published later this year by Trask House Press in Portland, Oregon, in conjunction with

Five Seasons Press in Hereford, by kind permission of the
poet's daughter Eleftheria Ritsou and of Kedros Editions, who
published the original text in February 1983.

5
I understood the trumpeter when I closed my eyes.

16
I saw you, and poems came back to me.

35
With your little finger you stir up a world.

60
Blood in the foundations of every bridge.

71
Voluptuary moon, don't take back what you said.

77
Let the dead sleep at last so we can sleep too.

78
Later the strip search of the corpses begins.

81
One mountain, two apples, three soldiers.

89
I entered the wooden horse with a sword and a mirror.

90
The beautiful corpse on its pyre, horse races, and the great
grief of the men.

104
They are afraid of his helmet, but not of his sword. He has
no sword.

105
They stoned him to death. With the rocks I built this
monument.

118
So formal was the uniform they dressed him in, he almost
lost his voice.

169
With her blue eyes she gives colour to the world.

184
They hauled down the flags. Went back to their homes.
They're counting their money.

193
The handsome boatman put a rose in Polydora's apron.

197
Breath of youth: the girl's breast wet from the ocean.

201
In young people's hands banners are singing.

205
Arethusa, holding the lyre on her Cretan lap.

209
A pale sleepwalker, wearing a red chrysanthemum.

219
Smashed marbles, restored with cement and plaster.

221
Beautiful dancer, don't say a word; dance.

241
Dawn. Myself and the sentry on the long bridge.

246
Your clothes, thrown down on the chair, still smell of the
ocean.

248
Yet another medal on your chest: yet another wrinkle on
your brow.

260
The lantern in the barracks where tired soldiers are asleep.

261
Shuttered house. Outside, the moon, and a sentry pissing in
the colonnade.

266
The flags' long strides, up high, above the young men's
shoulders.

Guillaume Apollinaire
Seven Poems
Translated by Stephen Romer

Of the translations, or transpositions, that follow, the first four are taken from Apollinaire's collection *Poèmes à Lou*, which was published posthumously in 1947, almost thirty years after the poet's death. The delay was due in part to the fact that the correspondence in which these poems are inserted had to be discovered, and in part due to the explicit nature of some of the material, all the more startling in its conflation of erotic conceit and martial imagery, the latter drawn spontaneously from Apollinaire's daily life as an artilleryman on the Champagne front. He served there from 1915 until he was wounded in the head on 17 March 1916, just a week after he was awarded French nationality. Apollinaire enlisted, and in April 1915 entrained north from Nîmes, bathed in the afterglow of a week of what appears to have been sweet and wild sexual ecstasy in the company of Louise de Coligny-Châtillon – 'Lou' – a young aristocratic beauty he had just met in Nice, and whose every aspect seemed to correspond point for point with the poet's ideal. The erotic pressure, a mixture of memory and desire, is unrelenting in the torrential letters and poems that he fired off to Lou in the weeks and months after their encounter. At their best, the poems draw into the vortex of longing the extraordinary sights and sounds of the Western Front; they are a wholly original mixture of French classicism in the style of the *blasons du corps feminin,* and modernist inclusiveness and invention. The *Poèmes à Lou* stand alongside the more famous *Calligrammes* in their 'celebration' – which is still startling to those accustomed to the poetry of protest of the British War Poets – of the 'matériel' of war. Not that Apollinaire was in any way duped, as the poem 'Cornflower' (written later, in 1917) makes clear. As for Lou, she replied more and more evasively to her lover's declarations; and after two brief leaves of absence early on in 1915, Apollinaire never saw her again, though the letters and poems continued until January 1916.

From *Poèmes à Lou*

X It's winter and already . . .

It's winter and already I've seen buds
On the fig trees in the little fields My love we're moving
Towards peace this springtime of the war where we are
We are at ease Down there listen to the cries of men
A Japanese sailor scratches his left eye with his right toe
On the road of exile are the sons of kings
My heart revolves around you like a troupe of
   young Serb soldiers dancing round
   a sleeping maid
The blond infantryman goes hunting lice in the rain
A Belgian interned in the Low Countries reads a paper
   with me in it

On the polder a queen stares with horror at the battlefield
The ambulance man shuts his eyes at the dreadful wound
The bell-ringer sees the belfry fall like an overripe pear
The English captain in the sinking vessel takes a last drag
   at his opium pipe
They cry Cry to the springtime peace that is coming
   Listen to the cries of men
But my cry goes out to you my Lou you are my peace and my
   springtime
You are my Lou darling the happiness I'm waiting for
It is for our happiness I prepare to die
It is for our happiness I still have hopes of life
For our happiness that the armies are fighting
That the decimated infantry
 appears in the range-finding mirror
That shells pass over like shooting stars
That prisoners march in dejected herds
That my heart beats only for you my darling
My love my Lou my art and my artillery

Xxxii (extracts) My Lou I shall sleep tonight . . .

My Lou I shall sleep tonight in the trenches
Freshly dug and waiting near our guns
Some twelve kilometers away are the holes
Where I shall go down in my coat of horizon-blue
Between the whizzbangs and the casseroles
To take my place among our soldier-troglodytes
The train stopped at Mourmelon le Petit
And I stepped down as happy as I climbed up
Soon we shall leave for the battery but for now
I'm among the soldiery and shells are whistling
In the grey north sky and no one thinks of dying . . .

. . . .

And thus we shall live on the frontline
And I shall liken your arms to the necks of swans
And sing your breasts belonging to a goddess
And the lilac shall blossom . . . I shall sing your eyes
Where a choir of lissom cherubs is dancing
The lilac shall blossom in the serious spring!

. . . .

Xxxviii My Lou my darling today . . .

My Lou my darling today I send you the first periwinkle
Here in the forest they've organized a wrestling bout
The men get bored alone without women and must be kept
   amused
On a Sunday
They've been cut off from everything for so long they hardly
      Know how to speak
Sometimes I'm tempted to show them your picture so that
      These young males
May look at your photograph
And remember what beauty is
But that is for me and only me
Only I have the right to speak to your portrait that is fading
To your portrait that is vanishing
Sometimes I look at it for ages one hour two hours
And I look at the 2 miraculous little portraits
      My heart
The battle for the sky drones on
Night has come
      How sad is the song in the depths of these nights
      Made by the shells revolving like worlds
So do you love me my heart and does your highborn soul
Want the laurel that decorates my head
I'll send along some myrtle some fine green myrtle

The crown of lovers who are uncorrupted
In the meantime I shall wear the oak
        The soldier's crown

And when shall I see you Lou my beloved
When shall I next see Paris and her pale light
Tremble on misty evenings around the streetlamps
When shall I see Paris and the smiles under little veils
The rapid little feet of unknown women
The tower of Saint Germain des Prés
The Luxembourg fountain
And you my adored one my uniquely adored one
You my darling love

Lxii Hill 146

No flowers left but strange signs
gesturing down the blue nights
in my prolonged adoration Lou
my whole being bows down
with the low clouds of July
before your memory

It is a white plaster head buried
helplessly next a golden ring
and our promises are remoter echoes
they sound sometimes strangely

There is a permanent white noise
my caustic solitude is lit up only
by the great searchlight my love
I can hear the bass voice of Big Bertha

And down by the trenches
in front of me a cemetery
has been sown
with forty-six-thousand soldiers
after such sowings we must
wait with serenity for harvest

                    If ever there were desolation
it is here where I write my letter
leaning on a slab of asbestos
I keep looking at your portrait
the one with the wide hat

Some of my comrades have seen your photo
and assuming that I know you
they ask who is she
and I can't quite think what to say
seeing as even now I hardly know you

Which pierces me
and deep inside the photograph
you are smiling still like light

Cornflower

Young man
Twenty years old
You have seen such horrors
What do you think
Of your childhood mentors now

You know
The bravura and the guile

You
Have
Seen
Death
Up
Close
More
Than
One
Hundred
Times
You
Do
Not
Know
What
Life
Is
Pass your braveness on
To those who come
After

Young man
You are joyful your memory is bloodied
Red too your soul
With joy
You have absorbed the life of those who died around you
You are decisive
It is seventeen hundred hours and you will know
How to die
If not better than your elders
More piously without a doubt
Since you know of death more than life
O sweetness of a different age
Agelessly drawn out

Postcard

I write to you under canvas
At the dying of this summer day
A blaze of artillery
In the faint blue sky
A dazzling bouquet
Fades before it was

Platoon Leader

My mouth will have the fires of Gehenna
My mouth will be a hell of sweetness and seduction
The angels of my mouth will lord it in your heart
The soldiers of my mouth will rout you
The priests of my mouth will cense your beauty
Your soul will tremble like salients in an earthquake
And then your eyes will brim
                        With all the love there ever has been
In human eyes from the beginning
My mouth will raise an army against you
An army of irregulars
Various like an enchanter who knows how to shift his shapes
The choirs and orchestras of my mouth will declare my love
(It murmurs to you from far away)
As I stand with my eyes fixed upon my watch
                Waiting for the moment we go over.

(Note: 'Cornflower' is taken from the posthumous collection *Il
y a* (1925), 'Postcard' and 'Platoon Leader' from *Calligrammes*
(1918).)

Pushkin
The Captain's Daughter
Extracts translated by Robert Chandler

The Captain's Daughter' is the subtlest of all nineteenth-century Russian novels. It is deeply poetic in texture, as well as containing a great deal of verse. The following pages contain my translation of all the chapter epigraphs and other poems, together with brief synopses of each chapter.

The Captain's Daughter

Take care of your honour when you are young.

1. A Sergeant of the Guards

A: *'He could be a captain in the Guards tomorrow.'*
B: *'No, no. Let him see service in the line.'*
A: *'Well said, well said – let a young man toil and sorrow!*
....
     And who's his father?'
Knyazhnin[1]

[The hero, Pyotr Grinyov, while still in his mother's womb, is enlisted in a prestigious Guards regiment. This was standard practice among the aristocracy; it enabled a young man to have seen enough years of 'service' by his late teens to have the right to join up as an officer. Pyotr's father, however, eventually decides that he does not want his son to lead the dissipated life of a young Guards officer in Petersburg. Instead, he sends him to serve in an ordinary regiment.]

2. The Guide

Land of mine, dear land,
Unknown land!
What brought me here was not my will,
What bore me here was not my steed,
What drew me here was reckless youth
And tavern wine.

                    Old Song

[1]Yakov Borisovich Knyazhnin (1742–91) was a poet, dramatist and civil servant. In this passage from his well-known comedy *The Braggart*, speaker B. is the father of the young man in question, though speaker A does not realize this.

[Lost in a snowstorm on his way to the fortress town of Orenburg, Grinyov is guided to a remote inn by a mysterious peasant. This peasant is as at home in the world of the steppe as Grinyov is lost in it. Grinyov shows his gratitude by giving him his own hareskin coat.]

3. The Fortress

Bread and water is our fare
In this fortress bleak and bare.
But if foes come, never fear,
We shall greet them with good cheer.
With powder, bullet, shot and shell
We shall feast them, feast them well.
Soldiers' Song

Old-fashioned people, sir!
Denis Fonvizin[2]

[Grinyov takes up his first posting, in one of the many small fortresses near the city of Orenburg, on what was then Russia's southeastern frontier. At first he is disappointed. What he had expected to be a grand and imposing place turns out to be little more than a village with a fence round it; and Captain Ivan Kuzmich Mironov, the fortress commandant, is far from the stern warrior of Grinyov's fantasies. Soon, however, Grinyov comes to appreciate the old-fashioned hospitality offered by the commandant and his family.]

4. The Duel

Since you've insulted me, or I have you,
You'll soon be seeing me run your body through.
Knyazhnin

---

[2]An eighteenth-century dramatist, famous, above all, for his comedy, *The Ignoramus.*

[Shvabrin, the other young officer in the garrison, speaks insultingly to Grinyov about Masha, the daughter of Captain Mironov. This leads to the two men duelling beside the river. Grinyov's aged servant, Savelich, runs down the steep bank, wanting to interpose his own body between Shvabrin's sword and his master's breast. His arrival distracts Grinyov and allows Shvabrin to wound him. The absurdity of this scene is anticipated in the epigraph, from a comedy called *The Eccentrics*. Two servants are about to fight a duel; this, of course, was something unthinkable – all the more so since they intend to fight with short knives.]

*

From lovely Masha I must flee,
No thought of love dare I confess,
For never may my heart be free
While I look on her loveliness.

But the eyes that first enchanted
Shine before me night and day.
By those lights this heart is haunted;
All sleep, all peace, they drive away.

Since I have divulged my anguish,
Dearest Masha, show compassion;
Or forever must I languish
In the grip of hopeless passion.

[A poem written by Grinyov. It is Shvabrin's criticisms of this poem that lead to his speaking insultingly of Masha.]

*

Captain's daughter, stay at home!
In the moonlight do not roam!

[Shvabrin drops these lines from a popular song into a
conversation with Masha's mother; only Grinyov is aware that
Shvabrin is casting aspersions on Masha's purity.]

*

5. Love

Maiden, maiden, pretty maiden,
Do not marry yet.
Ask your father, ask your mother;
Ask your parents, ask your kinsfolk.
Gather sense, gather wisdom;
There's no richer dowry.
                    Folk song

If you find someone better – you'll forget me.
Find someone worse – you'll remember me.
                    Folk song

[Grinyov and Masha fall in love. Grinyov writes to his father,
asking for his blessing on their marriage. The father refuses;
Masha is poor and their social inferior, and he is in any case
angry with Grinyov for having taken part in a duel. Masha
declares that she will never marry Grinyov without his parents'
blessing. Grinyov sinks into depression.]

6. The Pugachov Rebellion

Listen, young lads, listen well
To what we old folk have to tell.
Song

[Captain Mironov is informed that a rebellion has broken out
and that the rebel leader, Emelyan Pugachov, is likely to attack
Fort Belogorsk. The Pugachov rebellion (1773–75) was the
most serious of all Russia's popular rebellions. Pugachov wins
the support of several disparate groups of people: the peasantry
in general, Old Believers and other fugitives from imperial
authority, non-Russian nomadic tribespeople and the Cossacks
who were supposed to be defending the Tsar's fortresses and
stockades against these nomads.]

7. The Attack

Head of mine, steady head,
True and loyal soldier's head,
Three and thirty years you've served,
But you've never earned
Wealth or joy, praise or rank;
All you've earned, good head of mine,
Is two stout posts, a maple beam
And a noose of silk.
Folk song

[Pugachov captures Fort Belogorsk. He hangs Captain Mironov
and his wife but reprieves Grinyov at the last minute.
Pugachov turns out to be the peasant-guide of the second
chapter. He has spared Grinyov's life out of gratitude; he has
not forgotten his gift of a hareskin coat.]

8. An Uninvited Guest

An uninvited guest is worse than a Tatar.
                                        Popular saying

[Pugachov is, of course, an uninvited guest in Fort Belogorsk. The chapter title may also, paradoxically, refer to Grinyov, whom Pugachov commands to attend his victory feast. There is clearly a bond between Pugachov and Grinyov; Marina Tsvetaeva has argued eloquently that this strange bond is the most important love relationship in the novel.]

*

Don't rustle your green leaves, O green oak mother;
Don't let their sighs stop a young man from thinking.
For tomorrow, oak mother, this young man must stand
Before the sternest of judges, before the dread Tsar.
And the Tsar, dear mother, will ask me a question;
The Lord Tsar will say, 'Young son of a peasant,
Tell me about your companions, about your fellow thieves,
Tell me their number, tell me their names.'
And I shall tell you, my Lord, I shall tell you, my Tsar,
I shall tell you the whole truth:
My comrades, I tell you, were four:
'My blackest comrade was dark night,
My brightest comrade a steel knife,
My swiftest comrade was my brave steed,
My supplest comrade my taut bow,
And my messengers were piercing arrows.'
And my sovereign, my true hope, will reply,
'All praise to you, young son of a peasant,
That you thieve truly and that you speak true words.
And your reward, young lad, young son of a peasant,
Is a tall mansion in the open fields;
Your reward is two poles and a crossbeam.'[3]

[3]This song was popular among both peasants and Cossacks.

This simple song about the gallows, sung by men destined
for the gallows, had an extraordinary effect on me. Their
stern faces, their harmonious voices, the depth of feeling they
imparted to words in any case so very expressive – all this filled
me with ancient, poetic dread.

*

9. Parting

Meeting you, sweetheart,
Made my heart whole;
Leaving you, sweetheart,
Is the loss of my soul.

Kheraskov

[Freed by Pugachov, Grinyov leaves Belogorsk and Masha.
Masha, who has developed a high fever, has been taken in by
the priest and his wife. Not wanting Pugachov and his men to
know that she is Captain Mironov's daughter, they pass her off
as their niece.]

10. The Siege

Stationing his troops on hills and mountains,
He gazed like some fierce eagle on the town.
He hid his thunderbolts within huge engines
And when night fell he brought them to the gates.

Kheraskov

[Grinyov serves in the garrison of Orenburg, the provincial
capital. Pugachov besieges Orenburg for six months with an
army of at least 10,000 men. Pushkin's choice of epitaph is
ironical. Kheraskov was writing about how Ivan the Terrible
captured Kazan from the Tatars. In this chapter, however, it is
the Tsarist forces that are being besieged.]

11. The Rebel Camp

The savage lion was sated then.
'What means this visit to my den?'
He asked with gentle courtesy.
A. Sumarokov[4]

[Without permission from his commanding officer, Grinyov leaves Orenburg on horseback. He intends to ride to Belogorsk and rescue Masha. Pugachov has appointed the treacherous Shvabrin as the new commandant, and Shvabrin is trying to force Masha to marry him. Grinyov is captured by Pugachov's men and brought to his presence; this may have been Grinyov's secret hope.]

12. The Orphan

Our lovely apple tree
Has no young shoots and no fine crown;
Our lovely bride
Has no dear father and no dear mother.
No one to dress her
In a wedding gown,
No one to bless her.
                              Wedding song

[Grinyov has told Pugachov that he was going to Belogorsk in order to save his betrothed from Shvabrin. Furious to learn that Shvabrin is ill-treating an orphan, Pugachov takes Grinyov to Belogorsk with him; they sit side by side in Pugachov's sleigh. Pugachov reprimands Shvabrin and allows Grinyov and Masha to leave Belogorsk together. Grinyov sends Masha away to his

[4]These lines were in fact written by Pushkin himself, in the manner of Sumarokov (1717–74).

home, to be taken care of by his parents. He himself resumes
his military service.]

13. Arrest

'Duty, dear sir, requires that I compel
Your Honour to remain within this cell.'
'Duty, of course, is duty – I obey,
But first, dear sir, allow me too my say.'

[The campaign against Pugachov is nearing its end. Grinyov,
who is hoping that he will soon be able to marry Masha, is
arrested. Shvabrin, himself imprisoned for treason, has falsely
denounced him.]

14. The Tribunal

Man's fame –
Sea spume.
                    Popular saying

[Grinyov is found guilty by the tribunal. Masha travels
to Petersburg and petitions the Empress to show mercy to
Grinyov. She succeeds in clearing his name. They marry and
have children.]

Coats and Turncoats: A note on the poetry of *The Captain's Daughter*

In its overall structure the novel resembles nothing so much as
a fairy tale – or rather, two linked fairy tales. First Pyotr, and
then Masha, set out on their quests. Pyotr is a fairy-tale 'wise
fool'. As a child he is frivolous in his attitude to learning and,
in particular, to geography; he tries to turn a map of the world
into a kite. At an inn in the town of Simbirsk he gets drunk

and loses a lot of money; he then ignores his driver's warnings of a coming blizzard. Nevertheless he passes the crucial test, showing great generosity to a mysterious tramp – as much fairy-tale wolf as man – who emerges out of this storm, who seems almost to be born from it; and this wolf-man or – as we eventually learn – rebel leader, repays Pyotr's kindness many times over. Masha's quest is shorter but contains similar elements. Like Pyotr, she first speaks to her powerful saviour without realizing the saviour's true identity. And, like Pyotr, she reveals unexpected qualities; just as the seemingly foolish Pyotr succeeds because of his astuteness, so the seemingly timid Masha succeeds because of her courage.

Beneath the fairy-tale surface lies a deeply literary novel, full of quotation, pastiche and allusion. *The Captain's Daughter* can even be read as a discussion of the future direction of Russian literature. Pyotr has two tutors: one Russian and one French. At first Pyotr seems linguistically incompetent; he fails to learn French from Beaupré and, when he meets the incognito Pugachov in a remote inn, he is unable to understand his riddling Russian. In time, however, Pyotr grows to feel at home in both languages; he learns French, somewhat surprisingly, in a small fortress in the southeastern steppe and he develops a rapport with Pugachov. Pyotr's two languages, his two worlds, are represented by the epigraphs and embedded poems, half of which are drawn from folk song and half of which are examples or pastiches of elegant eighteenth-century verse. Pushkin may be suggesting that, like Pyotr, Russian literature can find its true path only by acknowledging both the Asiatic world of the steppe and the high culture of the elite.

Pushkin's apparently simple tale might, in fact, be in danger of collapsing under the weight and variety of its contents if it were not constructed with such elegant economy. This economy is not merely verbal. Every element in the novel does far more work than can reasonably be expected of it. The old cannon Pyotr glimpses on his arrival in Fort Belogorsk,

Captain Mironov's framed commission as an officer – these and many other objects, first introduced merely as background, come to play a part in the action. Pyotr's fencing lessons, his first encounter with Zurin and, of course, his readiness to give away a fine coat – all turn out to be more significant to the plot than the reader expects. The reader may, of course, guess that the gift of the coat will prove important, but he is unlikely to guess quite how often we will hear of this hareskin coat and from how many points of view.

The entire story *turns* on this coat, on Pugachov's *return* gift of a second coat, and on the ensuing allegation that Pyotr is a *turncoat*. This is not Pushkin's pun; I like to think of it, however, not as my own pun but as a small gift from the English language that a translator would be churlish to spurn. This play on words encapsulates the central themes of the novel and does something to compensate for my inability to reproduce the virtuosity of the word play – or sound play – of the original. An astonishing number of the most important and frequently used words in the novel are made up of permutations of the letters P, L and T. Clothes are *platye* and a coat is *tulup* or *pal'to*; a crowd is *tolpa*, a noose is *petlya*, a handkerchief (Pugachov waves a white handkerchief as a signal for his executioners to hang someone) is *platok*, and a raft (at one point Pyotr encounters a gallows on a raft) is *plot*; to pay is *platit'* and a half-rouble coin (first Pyotr tries, and fails, to give Pugachov half a rouble; then Pugachov tries, and fails, to give Pyotr half a rouble) is *poltina*; a rascal is *plut* and a crime is *prestuplenie*. Patronage is *pokrovitel'stvo* and to show mercy is *pomilovat'*. It is unlikely that anagrams have ever been used more subtly and with deeper meaning. Every element of sound and plot metamorphoses into another. The coat Pyotr gave Pugachov saves him from having a noose put round his neck in front of a crowd of rebels; the coat Pyotr receives from Pugachov leads to him being arrested by the Tsarist authorities.

The novel is a kaleidoscope – a true Joycean collidoscope.

Whole scenes are repeated, but seen in such a different light, at such a different angle, that we notice these repetitions only on reading the novel a second or third time. Zurin's peremptory letter demanding payment for a gambling debt is mirrored by Savelich's impertinent demand that Pugachov pay for the property that his men have stolen. As Pugachov's gift of a sheepskin coat mirrors Pyotr's gift of a hareskin coat, so Pugachov's failed attempt to give Pyotr half a rouble after allowing him to leave Fort Belogorsk mirrors Pyotr's failed attempt to give half a rouble to Pugachov at the inn. The verbal duel between Pyotr and Pugachov mirrors the actual duel between Pyotr and Shvabrin; all three men are, in a sense, poets, and a poem – or song – plays a part in each duel. And as Masha's silence when imprisoned by Shvabrin mirrors Pyotr's unexpected silence when accused of treason, so Masha's eloquent directness before Catherine the Great mirrors – and at the same time inverts – Pyotr's eloquent tricksiness before Pugachov. And as Pyotr saves Masha, so Masha saves Pyotr.

These parallels and inversions are more than a game; they hint at a crucial reality. The central parallel, after all, is that between Pugachov, a temporarily successful impostor, and Catherine the Great, the successful German pretender to the Russian throne. Catherine, we should remember, gained power by deposing her Russian husband, Peter III, the grandson of Peter the Great. The war between Catherine and Pugachov – who claims *to be* her murdered husband – embodies the split between Russia's westernized elite and its peasantry, two worlds that spoke different languages.

In reality, Pushkin, deeply sensitive to matters of honour, was killed in a duel occasioned by scandalous gossip about his wife. In the novel, the epigraph of which is 'Take care of your honour when you are young', Pyotr and Masha find a path to safety; together, they take care both of their honour and of their lives.

In 1917, the conflicts embodied in the novel were to tear Russia apart. At the level of art, however, Pushkin reconciles

these conflicts; no nineteenth-century Russian novel more
successfully brings together popular and high culture.

(Robert and Elizabeth Chandler's translation of *The
Captain's Daughter* is to be published by Hesperus in
June 2007.)

Vénus Khoury-Ghata
Six Poems from *Interments*
Translated by Marilyn Hacker

Vénus Khoury-Ghata is a Lebanese poet and novelist who has lived in France for the past thirty years. She is the author of sixteen collections of poems, including *Quelle est la nuit parmi les nuits* (Mercure de France, 2004) and *La Compassion des pierres,* (La Différence, 2001) and of as many novels, including *La Maison des orties* (Actes Sud, 2005) and *Une maison au bord des larmes,* translated by Marilyn Hacker as *A House at the Edge of Tears* (Graywolf Press, 2005). Two collections of her poems, translated by Marilyn Hacker, have appeared in the United States: *She Says* (Graywolf Press, 2003) and *Here There Was Once a Country* (Oberlin College Press, 2001). Other poems of hers, in Marilyn Hacker's translation, have appeared in the United Kingdom in *Poetry London, PN Review, Ambit* and *Banipal*.

(1)

To Andrei Makine

They salted the snow salted the lamb for the black banquet
placed a goblet on the roof for the moon's obol
locked up the water and the child who splashed the walls
    with their cries

They wrapped her in a sheet as rough as the salt marshes of
    poor seas
carried her on their shoulders with dregs of coffee and the
    cardamon favoured by angels
they gathered her

They crossed a desert two steppes three dunes and a valley so
    narrow they almost overturned her
then buried her backwards there where the earth's pulse
    stops
a sob's throw away from her kitchen
under the inconsolable carob tree
with the red washing-basin
and the cat's white meowing

They made her fly as high as a flock of goats from
    Mesopotamia
higher than bats
they forgot her

(2)

For Pierre Brunel

Sleeves rolled up
jackets hung from the walnut tree
several of them got down to work at ripping open the earth
placing the box in the red rectangle
at noon, sun and sweat

they ripped it open again by torchlight
neither in mourning nor need
their pickaxes' shadows drew a sextant on the cold grass
fire burned the night
night swept away the fire

they would have ripped it open at dawn with no north-point
    or landmark
if sleep had not gotten the better of arms and pickaxes

(3)

The bread-crumbs under the table are seeds of anger the old
    man scattered
he has overturned the day
overturned the hearth
closed his eyes to the cat lapping up the fire

The sky he says is a carpet burned by cigarette-butts
the earth is dead but doesn't know it yet
the earth is living on borrowed time

(4)

He has a rifle but no pencil
a long-lashed she-camel but no woman
on odd-numbered days his walls shrink down to a
    match-box

He goes to war when an Arab blackbird attacks his fig tree
makes the rounds of his field three times
swears that no word will leave his house alive

(5)

She is afraid to lose sight of her reflection
to no longer know what she looks like
to lose sight of her house
to no longer know if the door opens to the west
to learn that a road has gotten indoors
piled the chairs up on the table
that the plane-tree from the intersection is leaning on her
    railing

her fear of no longer knowing how to put out the sun
to evict the sob crowded into her throat

(6)

The map of the country was slashed from north to south
the postman delivered letters with no news
a botanist killed himself over a daffodil
which had forgotten his name

Only the foxes had memories
absent from the town hall registry
hens and cocks were listed in their notebook

in whose hand is my hand asked the woman in love
do you see our hearts in the mirror
why is it so dark under my dress?

Gilgamesh
An extract translated by Paul Batchelor

A Note About the Whole *Gilgamesh* Thing and a Translation of Tablet VI

Gilgamesh concerns the exploits of the warrior king Gilgamesh. His name means 'Our Ancestors were Heroes' and he protected his people by killing monsters such as Humbaba. That is, he protected his people when he wasn't raping or killing them: Gilgamesh has a claim to being the first tyrant, the first war criminal. Ishtar, goddess of love and war, was so impressed she tried to seduce our hero, who rejected her with this speech. In his efficiency as a slayer of monsters, Gilgamesh can be compared to later figures such as St George and Beowulf. His arrogant rejection of the Female throws an interesting light on the subtext of such myths; a Hughesian reading would be that this rejection *creates* the monsters with which he fights. The oldest story in the world readily finds contemporary resonances: Gilgamesh is king of Uruk, in what is present-day Iraq.

Finding an exact date for *Gilgamesh* is difficult because the poem is a composite of various tales from various periods. King Gilgamesh first appears in Old Sumerian narratives from ancient Mesopotamia: a scattering of songs and folk tales from the Early Dynastic period (mid-third millenium BC). The stories about his encounters with Ishtar are among the oldest extant texts. The creation of the more unified story we have today was a later, Babylonian achievement. My translation is from Tablet VI, which consists of manuscripts discovered in 1849 by Layard, in the South West Palace at Kuyunjik. These manuscripts are not Babylonian but Assyrian: three from Nineveh and two from Assur. Current thinking dates these manuscripts at mid-7th Century BC, though the story itself is much older. Discrepancies between different versions have given rise to many ambiguities over the precise meaning of certain words: did Ishtar turn Ishullanu into a toad, a spider or a scarecrow? We'll never know. Translators of *Gilgamesh* therefore rely on idealised, subjective, composite, variorum editions. They then make their own choices.

I became interested in *Gilgamesh* having read Stephen Mitchell's translation. This passage particularly appealed to me, so I compared Mitchell's with other versions and, as I became more interested, looked up a transcription of the original stone tablet at the British Library. As I am not familiar with the cuneiform alphabet, I relied on A. R. George's critical edition (OUP, 2003). This provides a transliteration, exegesis, commentary, a literal crib and a list of variations. I even found a phonetic approximation of what the thing would sound like. When I started work on my version, I tried to translate it into conventional English, but the longer I worked on it, the weaker it seemed. It took me about 18 months to realise the mess I was making. After that, I worked backwards, pushing the poem back towards the original and letting it keep its difficulties.

Gilgamesh Rebukes Ishtar

Tablet VI, lines 42-79

tell me one.   counting your lovers.   one you serve truly.
what of Tamuzzi.   how you love him.   dragging him down.
already bored.   calling nine demons.   nine women in Uruk.
beating their brows.   pet [lorikeet].   keening yet.
wings torn out.   how you love him.   hearing him grieve.
fourteen finding.   mountain lion.   cedar grove.
misused strength.   fluent weaponry.   digging a grave.
what of your lust.   battle-scarred stallion.   cursing the beast.
tasting the bit.   whip and spur.   galloping always.
bereft of sense.   how you love him.   queenly bequest.
piss in his waterhole.   goddess Silili.   endless disgrace.
what of your shepherd.   tender hand.   baking biscuits.
newborn lamb.   [buckling/bending].   making him butcher.
knuckled wolf.   how you love him.   dutiful son.
digging a trench.   dogs he trained.   trailing his scent.
last Ishullanu.   hungry eye.   figs and dates.
farmer's gifts.   [tilth/mulch].   gracing your table.
licked teeth.   breath in his ear.   'husbandman Ishullanu.
hold out your hand.   test how wet.   give me your cock.'
and he fearful.   'shall I fare.   scraps and slop.
shame and dishonour.   Ishtar's fare.   sow on her litter.
me with a home.   out in the wind.'   quickly broken.
trusted lovetricks.   so you serve him.   making him a toad.
poisoning his garden.   nothing grows.   were I your man.
will you deny it.   act in kind.   tell me the reason.
were I your sweet man.   counting your lovers.   my fate will be different.

Federico Garcia Lorca
'Song of the Civil Guard'
Translated by Mark Leech

In this 1926 poem, Lorca invents an assault on a gipsy city, but his writing reflects the real-life brutality and arbitrary cruelty of the Guardia Civil. This force, originally set up to police Spain's roads, had fallen under the control of local autocrats. Lorca may well have had the guardsmen of the Alpujarras, near Granada, in mind when writing this poem. Although written ten years before the outbreak of the Civil War, the extremity of the violence seems to prefigure much of that conflict, not least the summary execution of Lorca himself.

Horses, black, black horseshoes.
On the guardsmen's capes
gleam smears of ink and wax.
Their skulls are made of lead,
which is why they never weep.
With shined-up souls
they travel long roads,
hunchbacked, nocturnal.
Where they stop, they impose
the silence of dark rubber,
and fear, fine sand on the spine.
They go where they please
and carry in their heads
a vague astrology
of imagined guns.

                    *

Oh city of the gypsies,
banners on each corner,
moon and pumpkins, cherries
suspended in preserve.
Oh city of the gypsies
who could see you and forget?
City of musk and sorrow,
sweet with cinnamon towers.

                    *

When night came, night
All nighted up, deep night,
the gypsies in their forges
were shaping suns and arrows —
a horse, savagely cut,
hammered on each door.

Glass roosters sang all through
Jerez de la Frontera;
the wind came home naked
to the corner of surprise
in silvery silvery night
night all nighted up, deep night.

*

The Virgin and St Joseph
lost their castanets, and searched
for them among the gypsies.
The Virgin comes dressed up
in a mayor's wife's outfit,
bright chocolate wrapping
jewelled with almonds.
St Joseph shifts his arms
under a silky cape.
After him, Pedro Domecq
with three Persian kings.
The half-moon dreamed
an ecstasy of storks,
flags and lanterns storm
long terraces of roofs.
In the mirror, lacking hips,
dancers sob and sob.
Water and shadow, shadow
and water, all through
Jerez de la Frontera.

*

Oh city of the gypsies,
banners on your corners,
put your green lights out:
here come some *gentlemen*.

Oh city of the gypsies
who could see you and forget?

There let her stand, far from the sea,
her hair unpricked by combs.

        *

Two by two the guardsmen
come to the festive city,
a whisper of dead flowers
in their cartridge belts.
Two by two they come,
night redoubled in black cloth.
The sky's a bright showcase
of spurs – or so they like to think.

        *

The city free of fear
had many, many doors,
and forty Civil Guards
entered by them, to burn.

Clocks stopped short.
The cognac in its bottles
went frosty as November
so as not to draw their gaze,
and from the weathervanes
long flights of cries unreeled.

Sabres hack the breezes
that fall beneath the hoofs,
in shadowed streets old women
run and run and run
with their sleepy horses
and all their jars of coins.
Up the reeling streets
eerie capes advance
trailing rapid storms,
whirligigs of blades.

                    *

The gypsies gather
at the holy manger.
Joseph, clothed in wounds,
sheets a sweet girl.
Stubborn rifles snap
sharp words through the night.
The Virgin tends to children
with the spittle of a star.

The Civil Guardsmen
march like flames
to where, naked and young,
dreams are burned.

Rosa of Camborio
suffers at her door,
her severed breasts
bleeding on a tray.
Other girls run and run,
hunted by their tresses
in air blossoming
with guns' black roses.
When all the roofs were

trenched into the earth
stone-cold dawn shrugged,
re-took its ancient place.

*

Oh city of the gypsies . . .
Flames surround you.
The Civil Guards ride off
through a mine of silence.

Oh city of the gypsies
who could see you and forget?
They seek you on my brow,
a scene of moon, of sand.

Oliver Reynolds
'Kolin' and 'Dusty Miller Breaks his Silence' (after Liliencron's 'Wer weiss wo' and 'Vergiss die Mühle nicht')

Kolin
(18.vi.1757)

Soldiers drown in their blood.
Wheeling smoke, hoof-churned mud
   and the sheen
of a thousand spurs catches the sun.
No one's springing to attention
   at Kolin.

All the generals and squaddies
who necked bullets like toddies
   now stand easy.
Death having meant no harm
by his jogging each arm
   now stands easy.

An oblong bump in the shirt
of a corpse feeding on dirt
    looks like a book.
An adjutant stooped as he grieved
undid the pocket and retrieved
the Gospel of Luke.

Returned with Prussian palaver
to the high-ranking father
    fixed in his chair
it now bears a spidery inscription.
Kolin. My son lost in action.
    Who knows where.

And you who now read that line
are one with its writer: both decline
    to see what's there.
For each of us will be posted in turn
lost in action, to freeze or burn
    who knows where.

Dusty Miller Breaks his Silence

The marriage home
had just one view
an empty plain
where nothing grew

and all that moved
for miles of stone
was a windmill
that stood alone

turning slow sails
at the world's edge
windmill and wind
true to their pledge

Stephen Romer
Four Poems

Markie

'. . . but the grandest sight of the day was seeing the battalion advance, the men dancing along, only too anxious to get to close grips with the enemy. All behaved gallantly . . .' *King's Royal Rifle Corps Chronicle, 7th Battalion War Records, 1916*

Markie's pencil in the glass table,
with medals, cups, memorial coins,
knick-knacks of the drawing room

open to our silent curiosity
along with figs grown in hankies
and the coca-cola soda-maker...

MLRR, your initials, and your lost uncle's,
'mortally wounded' in 1916
between Longueval and Flers.

Scarcely spoken of, he wasn't shot
in front of your father's eyes
as family dramatics has it:

brothers were kept in separate trenches.
His details were waiting
on the War Graves website,

Name/Rank/Regt/Battalion/ —
and we are the 'third generation',
grandsons to process memories . . .

'There's a lot of interest now'
goes the chirpy voice on the telephone
in answer to my inquiry.

'He mightn't have died in a major assault,
it could have been sniper, accident,
anything . . .' 'That's OK' I replied.

His parents received the Field Postcard,
the 'wounded' line applies.
His mother's day-book stops.

Armistice

The unnatural
shopper-and-traffic halting
silence.
Wizened scarlet pennants
shiver and rattle once.

The air is sootfall
a glowering tree-line
drawn to attention
and monochrome
between branches.

A sickly afforestation
to the East
the 'sacred acreage'
that 'altar copiously asperged'.
A yearlong harvest

has arrested nature
who else swallows
all things up,
Assurbanipal of Nineveh
his engines.

Stand-To

'Jardin où saigne abondamment le laurier rose fleur guerrière . . .'
— Apollinaire

This garden everywhere
is transfigured for minutes on end
after rain, a breach in the west,
russet light solid on trees and walls

and on the squat church tower.
How many did the village lose?
Evening after evening, bearing arms
against the afterglow,

he missed the church bell, and the harvest
in the vineyard overhead
the year of the heat-wave
that killed the old, the year of the *grand cru.*

He comes home, at this moment, pauses
in this precise light, and then
descends the stone steps
slowly as from a podium.

XI/XI/XI

The jolly octogenarian
with a face like Louis de Funès, gone scarlet
behind his trumpet
this ninetieth anniversary of the Marne
is known as *une mémoire.*
His father led the village fanfare
now blaring out the Marseillaise
in the blanched church,
cold and too big for our gathering . . .

Cold as the chapels
of Père Lachaise, preceding the crematoria,
cold and grandiose, it's a kind of genius.

He draws me in, the newcomer,
for a bit of friendship, *nom de dieu!*
Dans l'instruction publique, il paraît?

Thus I am enrolled in the Republic.

After 'eighteen, the village declined,
artisans, wine merchants, masons, butchers,
marriages, alliances, neighbours.
So-and-so's father lost his toes,
trench feet in the Ardennes. Widows
and orphans. Over the river
is a windowless village called Veuves.

*   *   *

Ivy crowds the gable, wisteria
burrows beneath the tile
and breaks the roof, the place is ruined.
A hollow in the bed marks where she died.
In the freaks and squibs of November light
a thin wind shakes the creeper.
It whimpers through a planted forest
of withered saplings.

The eleventh hour the eleventh day
how far can colour drain away
and still remain colour?
The blueish tinge of birth and death
and the *poilu's* frozen gills
has seeped into the world,
with words like *blême, blafard, blanchâtre* . . .
Corridors of a military hospital
for men whose faces have been blown off,
nurses descending like gulls or ghouls
in their long white robes and veils
ministering to the noseless
wheeling the cripple in his chair
through a courtyard with ambulances.

White-smocked doctors at Berck,
kindly-stern,
the chafing of prosthetics.

Exsangue, the horrified angel
with the staring eyes, and her fingers
on her lips, saying 'Hush!'
in the chapel of remembrance.

Around the monument
the wind pierces and the struggling leaves
on the tops of poplars fly away
Mort pour la France, as every name is called
in the roll of glory.
The bloodied tricolore
is topped with a spike.

              *   *   *

How talkative they are! So much to remember
and no one very much to listen,
an aged genial gathering, facing up
to the unpromising municipal grey.
Over a glass of *champenoise*
a brother-in-law chatters on
gobbets of his canapé
landing in my glass
-how the girls would cycle
daily to Amboise
before they built the HLM.

Unfathered, unbrothered, unhusbanded,
the girls in their scarves, brave smiles
on bicycles, heading off
and homing with the angelus,
that is ringing now, calling us
to the immutable, sacred hour of lunch.

Du Fu
Two Poems
Translated by Paul Harris

Du Fu (712–770, also known as Tu Fu) wrote during what is usually regarded as the golden age of Chinese poetry, the Tang Dynasty, more specifically the reign of the emperor Ming Huang ('Brilliant Emperor'). While ostensibly about the hardships caused by the expansionary territorial policies of an earlier dynasty, the 'Ballad of the Military Waggons' is probably meant to be a criticism of the military ambitions of Ming Huang himself. A few years after its composition, Du Fu himself experienced war first-hand. In 755 a former court favourite called An Lushan started a rebellion, which led to the emperor fleeing the capital, Chang'an (present-day Xi'an). In the ensuing confusion the city was the scene of looting and, when later occupied by rebel troops, great slaughter. An Lushan was later assassinated in a conspiracy in which his own son was implicated. The Tang was eventually restored in the person of Ming Huang's third son and continued for another 150 years, but it never recovered its former power and prosperity. Du Fu seems not to have witnessed the fall the Chang'an, but he saw its aftermath, possibly as a prisoner-of-war of the rebel army. Like most Chinese poets, Du Fu was also a civil servant (though of modest rank) and so could have been considered potentially useful to a fledgling new government. 'Scene in Spring' evidently describes a personal reaction to this disaster, with a touch of self-deprecatory humour at the end.

Despite his being often referred to as the greatest Chinese poet, a relatively small proportion of Du Fu's work is accessible in English. This may be because the qualities of compression and potential ambiguity of the Chinese literary language and the formal complexity of its verse forms are exploited to the full in much of his verse, and these present a formidable barrier to effective translation. Since a literal rendering of the words would often be meaningless in English, the end result of any attempt to be true to the spirit of the original will always involve a degree of re-interpretation of the poem in question.

Ballad of the Military Waggons

The waggons rumble and creak, horses snort and whinny.
The marching men all carry a bow and arrows at their waist.
Fathers, mothers, wives, children run by their sides, seeing
 them depart,
While swirls of dust blot out the view of Xianyang bridge.
Tugging at the clothes of their loved ones, stamping their
 feet in protest, they cry out and weep.
The sound of weeping rises to the very heavens.
To the question from a passer-by on the roadside,
All the men can say is: They are levying soldiers, Sir.
Some of us were sent north at fifteen to defend the Yellow
 River region.
And even at forty we have to go west to man the farms and
 grow the food.

When we left, we were so young the old people had to fasten
   our headwear for us.
When we came back, our hair was white, and we still have
   to go and defend the frontier.
On the frontier it's like a sea of blood.
But the Emperor still means to extend his lands.
Haven't you heard, Sir, how all the villages round about are
   overgrown with thorns and brambles?
Though the women are strong and know how to handle a
   hoe and drive a plough,
The grain grows all over the place.
Because they know the soldiers of Qin will put up with
   anything,
We're herded around no better than dogs or poultry.
'Why do we let them?', you ask. We don't dare complain.
Take this winter, you see, they need even more of us,
While the county officials press for more taxes.
I ask you, where is it all to come from?
People say now it's better to give birth to daughters. Having
   sons is nothing but trouble.
At least you can marry a daughter to a neighbour.
But a son will only end up six feet under.
Do you know, far away by the Kokonor,
Where for ages and ages soldiers' bleached bones have lain
   uncollected,
New ghosts now come to haunt those who have gone before,
While the wet wind wails against a surly sky.

A Scene in Spring

The state is torn apart, only the mountains and rivers
   remain.
Weeds and trees run rampant in the city this spring.
Do the flowers sense the times, that they, like me, should
   weep?
Do the birds feel the emptiness, they seem so fearful?
For three months on end the garrison beacons have
   glimmered at night.
A letter from home would be worth a heap of gold to me,
An old man waiting, whose remaining white hairs
Will soon become too sparse even to hold a hat pin.

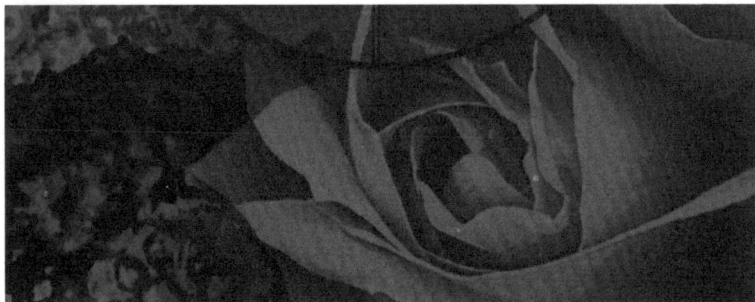

Charles Dobzynski
'My Life as a Wall'
Translated by Marilyn Hacker

Charles Dobzynski was born in Warsaw in 1929; his parents migrated to France in 1930. In hiding during the war, which interrupted his schooling, he published his first poem in *Jeune Combat*, a journal originating in the Jewish Resistance, in 1945. Today, he is the author of some forty collections of poems, including *Corps à réinventer* and *Le réel d'à côté* (both 2005) and *À Revoir la mémoire* (2006). He is also the editor and translator of the Gallimard Anthology of Yiddish Poetry, and the emeritus editor-in-chief of the journal *Europe*, for which he continues to write a monthly poetry review column. He was named a Chevalier des Arts et Lettres by the French Cultural Ministry, and received a fellowship from the Académie Goncourt for the totality of his work.

My Life As a Wall

For Israël Eliraz

Neither alive nor dead I am a wall
between two lands
a mouth between two tongues.

*

Not something which offers what can be shared
like birth
but something that separates forever.

*

Not a border
but a moat to hinder
human connections.

*

The tsunami of a glance
is a permanent danger
for those who refuse to see.

*

A wall between two countries
like a dagger
between two ribs.

*

A wall is always something
like a prison
I imprison horizons.

*

I am a wall and I suffer
my cement condition
enclosure is my punishment

*

Yard after yard I forge
the bolt
which locks being from being

*

A wall between two countries
one myopic, the other one-eyed
each one ogling the other.

*

The land on the wrong side
engulfed
in the imago of settlements.

*

Those bulldozed houses
a reassurance
for the Sabbath feast.

*

Dismembered zones
the bones will be gathered
when the body disappears.

*

Only Life, clear-sighted,
looks right through the stones
without understanding.

*

What am I but a wall
who, in my hollows,
holds cries?

*

A wall who wails
at having to be
what it is.

*

A wall whose only
hope is its own
destruction.

*

A wall on one side of which
life is full
and on the other still empty.

*

A wall which has on one side
the power
of a State

*

And on the other
the weakness
of destitution.

*

I am a wall which even
the rain avoids
in shame.

*

A wall where the sun
scratches itself in vain in search
of its memory.

*

A wall with no identity
but fear on one side
and hatred on the other.

*

A wall with an unbroken view
in black and white
of human misfortune.

*

With this wall, they built me
the Yad Vashem
of a new annihilation.

*

How can you be a Jew when a wall
cuts you in two
when a wall takes away your history.

*

When a wall breaks the link
with that other who is yourself
or will become you.

*

For each of us is someone's Jew
if we refuse
to be his wall of blindness.

*

The Just do not inhabit
only one hemisphere
of speech.

*

There are those who have neither asylum
nor labour
if not with the master.

*

The wall is the bloody signature
of a war
in which no crime is pardoned.

*

Neither the razed houses
nor the bombings
so many broken lives.

*

I am a wall without answers
who exudes only the tears
of my past.

*

The wall is victim
of what it tried to prevent:
death does not lay down its weapons.

*

The wall between those who kill
has no meaning or future
except to come down.

*

I am a wall who, at night,
weeps for all the victims,
their hope vanished.

*

The wall knows nothing it sweats
blood and water memory
its height is not a way out.

*

The wall forbids me to be wholly
a Jew
like a grave-digger.

*

Jump over my wall
over my dream
which is to die.

*

To die by euthanasia
for you on one and on the other side
of my prison.

Stephanie Norgate
'Aulis'
A haiku version of Lucretius' *De Rerum Natura*, Book 1, lines 80-101

After some experimentation with various block forms, I found the haiku a rewarding option, though it may seem an odd choice for a didactic argument. I noticed that clauses such as 'fluctifrago suspensae in litore vestes/uvescunt' or 'stilicidi casus lapidem cavat' are almost the syllabic length of haiku and work through a similar economic expression of image. To create the sense of argument, I've allowed myself some enjambement, questions and links not normally found in haiku. This became part of the translation process – of form as well as meaning. Sometimes I have transferred significances associatively e.g the reference to Hymen in 'Aulis' becomes a distorted wedding scene, *hymns, his men* and so on. Lucretius' addressee Memmius, is known as Mem, as this diminutive suggested a contemporary relationship (also perhaps because one senses Lucretius arguing with himself). I have kept Iphianassa for the sound despite losing the dramatic shadow of Iphigenia.

(Note: There will be more of Stephanie Norgate's haiku
Lucretius in our next issue.)

Aulis

'More often religion, rather than reason, gives birth to
violence.' (*DRN* Book 1 ll.80-101)

Mem, I fear your fear –
that embarking on reason
is somehow sinful.

But think of Aulis –
how the Greeks spilt a girl's blood.
Iphianassa

dressed for a wedding,
ribbons hanging from her hair,
trembled up the aisle

to meet her father.
The minister hid the sword.
The crowd was crying.

She fell on her knees,
silenced by fear, was hauled
forward by his men.

No husband. No hymns.
No peal of bells. No 'I do'.
Idolatry. Yes,

her father felt grim
but, in war, the fleet comes first.
To leave port safely

they must pray, must pay,
must give away some dear thing.
The unseen goddess

loves the iron smell,
loves bribes, smoke. So they say.
His blood. Hers. Her breath

rattling in the masts,
blood shimmer of ore flushing
round the keels. Blade. Skin.

Iphianassa
splattering down the altar.
War boats on water.

There, Mem.
            You see how
such blind faith can lead a king
to kill his daughter?

Robert Desnos
Ten Poems
Translated by Timothy Adès

Robert Desnos, 1900–45, was the most exciting and skilful French poet of his time. He first delighted the Surrealists with his spontaneous super-Spoonerisms by 'Rrose Sélavy'. Of his love-poems, the first below were among those he wrote for the chanteuse Yvonne George. She did not respond and around 1929 he found lifelong love with Youki Foujita (Lucie Badoud). The poems for Yvonne tended to be in free verse; those for Youki were at first childlike, then longer and more formal.

He wrote magnificent poetry during the Occupation, with pseudonyms or literary allusions to beat the censor. Arrested in 1944 as a Resistance man, after a year of slave labour he died at Terezin. For his supposed 'last poem', see below. In his real last poem he returned to Rrose Sélavy, but in the sonnet form.

From *Corps et Biens,* 1953

I've dreamed of you so much

for Yvonne

I've dreamed of you so much that you lose your reality.
Is there still time to reach that living body and to kiss on
    those lips the birth of the voice I love?
I've dreamed of you so much that my arms, which always
    find my own breast even as they clutch at your shadow,
    may never close on the contours of your body.
So much that, confronted by one who has haunted and
    controlled me for days and for years, I would certainly
    become a shadow myself.
O sentimental scales.
I've dreamed of you so much that it's probably no longer
    time I woke up. I'm asleep on my feet, exposing my body
    to all the experiences of life and love, and as for you, the
    only woman who matters to me today, I'd be less able to
    touch your lips and brow than the first lips and brow to
    come along.
I've dreamed of you so much, walked, talked, lain with your
    phantom so much that all that's left to me, perhaps, is to
    be a phantom among phantoms and a hundred times more
    shadowy than that shadow walking in joy, now and in
    time to come, across the sun-dial of your life.

*The last sentence, slightly altered, is inscribed on the Monument to the
Martyrs of Deportation, behind Notre-Dame, at the tip of the island.
It had come back from Terezin, translated into Czech, and was taken
to be an unknown, final, patriotic message.*

'Ce Coeur Qui Haïssait La Guerre' is also quoted there. Robert Desnos
is the only writer to be honoured at the Monument with two
quotations.

No, love is not dead

No, love is not dead in this heart and these eyes and this
    mouth that declared its funeral had begun.
Listen, I've had enough of the picturesque, of colours and
    charm.
I love love, its tenderness and cruelty.
My love has only one name, only one form.
All passes. Mouths are pressed to that mouth.
My love has only one name, one form.
And if one day you remember,
You, form and name of my love,
One day on the sea between America and Europe,
At the time when the sun's last ray rebounds from the
    water's wavy surface, or on a stormy night under a tree in
    the country or in a fast car,
A spring morning in the Boulevard de Malesherbes,
A rainy day,
At dawn before you went to bed,
Tell yourself (I command your familiar phantom) that only I
    loved you more, and it's a pity you didn't know.
Tell yourself one must have no regrets: Ronsard before me
    and Baudelaire sang the regrets of old women and dead
    women who spurned the purest love.
You when you are dead
Will be beautiful, still desirable.

I shall be dead already, all enclosed in your immortal body,
   in your wondrous image present for ever among the
   perpetual wonders of life and eternity, but if I live
Your voice and its rhythm, your gaze and its radiance,
The scent of you and of your hair and more besides will live
   in me,
In myself who am neither Ronsard nor Baudelaire,
Myself, Robert Desnos, who by having known and loved you
Am their equal;
Myself, Robert Desnos, by loving you
And I wish to add no other report to my memory on this
   pitiful earth.

Never another but you

Never another but you for all the stars and solitudes
All the trees hacked at nightfall
Never another but you shall trace her path which is mine
The more you recede the bigger your shadow
Never another but you shall greet the sea at dawn when I
   emerge leg-weary from the dark forests and nettle-patches
   and make for the foam
Never another but you shall put her hand on my brow and
   my eyes
Never another but you. I deny falseness and infidelity
That anchored ship you can cut its rope
Never another but you
The eagle shut in a cage slowly gnaws the verdigris-green
   copper bars
What an escape!

It's Sunday marked by nightingale-song in fresh green
   woods the boredom of little girls at a fretting canary's
   cage, while slowly in the lonely street the sun moves its
   thin line across the hot pavement
We shall pass other lines
Never never another but you
And me alone alone alone like faded ivy in suburban gardens
   alone as glass
And you never another but you.

From *Destinée Arbitraire*, 1963/1975

Beautiful After-Midnight

for Youki

Whiter than the snow or the crystals of salt
Flowers of night are spreading wide their petals
Growing in the sky to fill the spaces of the vault
Where a blue horse neighs, kicks, heads for meadows

And grasslands sown with newly minted stars
Through harvests of pinpoints and reflected light
Spattering the sails with its four horseshoes' flares
Plunging in deepest shadows milky-white

Rolling out the ribbon of rhythms long since dead
The shortest buckling with the weight of day's last fire
Suns paled and faded that went too near the red
Glow of the constellations Hercules and Lyre

Even now the moon who is robed as a bride
Drags in her white claws the misty one and white
White as the morning on ocean petrified
The ram of the dawn prepares his dashing flight

The comet is wearing its sparklers on its brows
You moon black and beautiful moving slow ahead
Where do you meet your golden-plum-eyed spouse?
With a splendid body Venus warmed his bed

You champagnes go streaming through the constellations
If wines are similar to liquid stars
Then Burgundy in you let's recover the creation
Of fairytale monsters, the ether, empty spheres.

Cancer and the Bear, Mercury and Jupiter,
As we press the vintage we shall make them shine
Never mind the sun bathed in fresh spring-water
Never mind the torches reflected in the wine

Beautiful after-midnight with the legends in your train
Draw another couple to the waltzes of desire
Till the weary drinker shall ask you once again
To fill up his glass with blood of memory's fire!

Bagatelles

You'll come back to me, she said,
Rich as Croesus, when the rose
Down at Bagatelle shall spread
Buds and blossoms in the snows.

Washing loads of river-sand,
Breaking quartz to smithereens
Tapping rubber from a stand
Of infernal round-boled trees

Freeing up the beds of oil
Heavy work in the Alaskas
Eighty years in yielding soil
Hidden treasure of the Incas

He came back but she'd passed over.
He was old and cretinous.
Even so, this type of lover,
They are hardly numerous.

May there bloom at Bagatelle
Roses of the snow and frost
May those darlings bloom as well
That we love till life is lost.

Song of the Glass of Wine

When the train goes don't wave your hand,
Your handkerchief, your umbrella,
But fill a glass with wine,
And throw, towards the train whose grab-rails are singing,
The wine's long flame,
The wine's bloody flame that is like your tongue,
And shares with it
The palate and the couch
Of your lips and your mouth.

Song of the Butcher

If you like, my beauty, I'll make your bed
In my shop's interior, bloody-red.
My knives shall be the magic mirrors
Where the daylight rises, flares and flickers.
I'll make your bed hollow and hot
In a heifer's slitted gut
To restore your youth. While you sleep I'll watch it
Like an executioner wielding his hatchet.

Seasons

Day is in place, runs down as time expires,
Unless one soars through the successive layers
Of a recall that disencumbers, clears
The heart and brain of clinging souvenirs.

Great summers, *étés*, even your name goes past,
Now *is*, now *has-been*, pastimes, primes of years,
Tireless as water it goes past, has passed,
Leaving no pools, no witnesses, no scars.

Seasons, at least you nurse the corn, the grain
That burgeons in the thaw, you have the key
That opens gates for wagonloads to leave.

You bring the stars together in the sky.
The year will soon be done: tired footsteps heave
Down trails that lead to frontiers, back again.

Tomorrow

I'd live a hundred thousand years, and still
Be staunch in hope's foreknowledge of the dawn.
Old Father Time, whom sprains and shocks make ill,
Can moan – the dusk is new, new is the morn.

Too many months by now we've been on guard.
Alert, we've kept our firelight and our flame,
Talked low and pricked our ears at noises heard
That soon fell silent, lost, as in a game.

Now from night's fastness we attest again
The splendour that accompanies the day.
Unsleeping, we are watchers for the dawn,
Proof that, at last, we are alive today.

Springtime

(The real 'last poem', 6 April 1944)

Rrose Sélavy, beyond these bounds you stray.
Meanwhile the waters and the earth ferment;
The rose on fortress-walls pours out its scent;
Love has its sweats and springtime is their prey.

The rose has torn the stone-limbed dancer's side.
While others plough and sow, he treads the boards.
The public, blind and deaf and dumb, applauds
This rite of spring, when he has danced and died.

The word that's writ in soot is wiped away
At the wind's whim by fingers of the rain.
Nevertheless we hear it and obey.

Down at the wash-place where these waters run,
A cloud portrays both soap and hurricane,
Retreating when the thickets bloom in sun.

The Corneliu M Popescu Prize
for European Poetry Translation 2007

Image: 'The Confusion of Tongues', Gustave Doré. With thanks to Rev. Felix Just, S.J.

Sponsored by the Ratiu Family Charitable Foundation

Judges: Anne Born & Francis Jones
Prize: £1,500
Closing date: 31 May 2007

The prize is open to collections of poetry published between April 2005 and May 2007 which feature poetry translated from another European language into English.

Submissions should be sent to Translation Prize, The Poetry Society, 22 Betterton Street, London, WC2H 9BX. Three copies of each book should be sent. Proof copies will be accepted and the original language(s) of the poems should be specified.

For further information telephone 020 7420 9880
or email competition@poetrysociety.org.uk
www.poetrysociety.org.uk /
www.ratiufamilyfoundation.com

THE POETRY SOCIETY

THE RATIU FAMILY
CHARITABLE FOUNDATION

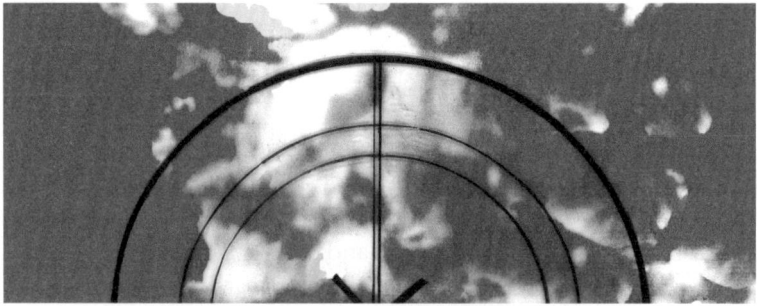

Anzhelina Polonskaya
Four Poems
Translated by Andrew Wachtel

Anzhelina Polonskaya was born in Malakhovka, a small town near Moscow. She began to write poems seriously at the age of eighteen. At that time she was a professional ice-show skater. Between 1995 and 1997 she lived in Latin America, working as an ice dancer. Her first book of verses *Svetoch Moy Nebesny* (My Heavenly Torch) appeared in 1993.

In 1998, the Moscow Writer's Publishing House published her second book, entitled *Stikhotvoreniia* (Verses). Having left the ice show, Polonskaya decided to devote herself to literature. Since 1998, she has been a member of the Moscow Union of Writers.

In 2004 an English-language collection, entitled *A Voice*, appeared in the *Writings from an Unbound Europe* series at Northwestern University Press. This book was shortlisted for the 2005 Corneliu M Popescu Prize for European Poetry in Translation. Polonskaya's work has also been translated into Dutch and Spanish.

Polonskaya continues to live and work in Malakhovka, where she is preparing a new volume of poetry for publication.

Two Birds

Two birds on the gray, ashy sand.
The sleeping bird is on the right; her feathers are dull
and forgetting has prepared a place for her in the fallen
    leaves.
The wind tears a feather from her wing, to write
in the rain's invisible ink the word Umbra
on one side and Lumen on the other, over where
the second bird cries over the dead one, opening its yellow
    beak.
Sending you this picture, I only want to say
that I can be both birds at once.

Flavia

Every day I return to you, my Flavia.
Your horse has died and a crowd of barbarians wanders in
    my rebellious thoughts.
Every time my naked muse shares my bed
I remember your hands on my clothes
under the stars twinkling over the Bosporus.
Then you became a general, Flavia,
brave and wise Flavia, the empress's loyal man.
In the nights I heard the banging of stones
as a wall was raised around me.
Could they really have been the same hands?

Leaves

Like lost children, the dry leaves
on the mournful sidewalks
wind around our legs.
Could those fallen leaves
ever find their mother
under this autumn sky?
Perhaps a bird, tired of flying,
giving in to nature's ancient laws,
will entrust to them her dull wing.
Or, while speaking with you,
I will turn an accidental glance
toward that quiet arboreal rot,
more indifferent even
than God's indifference.
The wind blows the leaves away.

Ship of the Universe

Dawn. The lights of the infinite
ship of the universe have gone out,
the cups are drunk to the dregs
and the tyrants all beheaded—
on the executioner's block
a trident of bird traces
and a blanket of fog.

The pages are shredded
and on the walls
a horde of shadows.
With its last beams
a moonlit child plays on the white
hills of your knees
and a beam melts in your elbow's bend.

Doleful eyes awake,
they look and see
souls,
the flotsam of that universe,
blown ashore,
and a star that blinks in the murk,
following the ship's masts.

Manuel Rivas
Six Poems
Translated by Jonathan Dunne

Manuel Rivas is internationally Galicia's best-known author. His short novel *The Carpenter's Pencil*, a love story set in the Spanish Civil War, is the most widely translated novel written in Galician and prompted Günter Grass to comment that he learned more about the Spanish Civil War from reading this novel than from any history book. The English translation was a recommended read in Waterstone's during January 2001.

Manuel Rivas was born in Coruña on the coast of Galicia, Spain, in 1957. He writes in Galician, together with Spanish, Catalan and Basque an official language and the second most widely spoken minority language in Europe after Catalan and before Welsh. He is a regular contributor to the Spanish daily *El País* and other newspapers. He has published six novels, six collections of short stories and a beautiful play called *The Hero*. His poetry has been collected in *From the Unknown to the Unknown* (2003), an extensive selection of which has been translated into English and is awaiting publication.

Already published in English are his novels *The Carpenter's Pencil* (2001) and *In the Wilderness* (2003), nominated for the International IMPAC Dublin Literary Award and the

Weidenfeld Translation Prize respectively, and his short-story collection *Vermeer's Milkmaid & Other Stories* (2002). The author lived in London from 1999 to 2000 on the trail of migrants' stories and, during this time, *Butterfly's Tongue*, a film based on three short stories, was distributed in the UK, which saw both author and translator tour various cinemas in London and Cambridge. Since then, a film has also been made of *The Carpenter's Pencil*, directed by the Galician rock star Antón Reixa.

Manuel Rivas founded Greenpeace in Spain and spearheaded the very public protests over the *Prestige* oil spill off Galicia's coast in 2002 and the Spanish government's handling of the catastrophe. These included the congregation of 100,000 protesters with empty suitcases in Santiago de Compostela's main Obradoiro Square.

Manuel Rivas' most recent publication is the 700-page thriller *Books Burn Badly*, which has books as its protagonists.

Ballad on the Western Beaches

The ship settles on the shore
and land birds nest on its mast.
With the compass I trace routes on maps of tillage,
hurt by the sky's anger on the seed's weak ribs,
fearful of the flower's drift before inhumane winds.
The ship sleeps on the shore,
the keel's blue imagination covered in brush and rushes,
and the figurehead has a strolling soul.
In the binnacle is kept the book of moons and the rains'
    needle,
a bottle of old snow liqueur.

A skylark sings on a rusty harpoon,
a blackbird's sigh lashes the cables
and crows on the rudder glimpse lesser death lying
    alongside.
All set, admiral, for the great journey.

Radiophony

Were death to speak,
were it something more than a smell,
it would make this noise:
that of an oar beating against the skin of the void.
I sometimes think I hear it at sea,
between news items extinguished like lights.
The sea is an old radio,
the embrace of a grandfather who became a poet of silence.
The din of your startled horses reaches here,
the anguished neighs of battle.
Your orders reach here,
your sons' laments,
the creaking of the cage.
It's like a falling guffaw,
the beat of an oar against emptiness.
Songs sometimes reach here,
a dance of silks,
and the sea whirls and whirls like an old mystic.

The Milkmaid

for Carmen from Corpo Santo, who brought me up

Centuries ago, mother, in Delft (remember?)
you were tipping the jug in the home of Johannes
Vermeer, the painter, husband of Catharina Bolnes,
daughter of Mrs Maria Thins, that uptight lady,
who had a half crazy son,
Willem, if my memory does not fail me,
who dishonoured poor Mary Gerrits,
the maid now opening the door
for you, mother, to enter
and go to the table in the corner
and from the jug pour the luminous butterflies
your family's cattle grazed
in Delft's green, sombre rags.
Just as I dreamt it in the Rijksmuseum,
Johannes Vermeer with milk will whitewash
those walls, the brass, the wicker, the bread,
your arms,
though in the fiction of the painting
the source of light is the window.
Vermeer's light, that enigma of centuries,
that ineffable clarity shaken from God's hands,
milk drawn by you in the dark shed,
in the bats' hour.

Tenderness

Seeing man on his own,
weary,
his hoofs in the snow,
ermined in stars,
howling towards the infinite

Red Rose, Proud Rose, Sad Rose

I knew some men who carried the red flag
when it was a sin and beautiful
like a holly berry.
I myself held one, a red flag, in my hands
when it was a sin and beautiful
like a stork's beak.
I've heard of men in Calcutta and Soweto
who still carry red flags,
beautiful like camellias between the teeth.
But I didn't want today to tell you
of the proud, red and sad flag
that heated the hands of those underneath,
a sin and beautiful like a coal flame.
I only wanted to tell
of the holly berry,
the stork's beak,
the camellia between the teeth,
the coal flame
and the proud, red, sad Rose of Yeats.

The Last Judgement

Riseth ye up that ben ded, and cometh to the jugement
Chaucer

And so God will send the angels
to separate the good from the bad.
And they will put some to one side with the saint Abel,
the martyrs
and the beggar Lazarus.
The others with Cain,
the blustering tyrant
and the rich glutton.
On the right Peter and on the left Judas
the infamous.
Till when? the damned will ask.
And the Lord will clear his throat with a glass of water:
For ever and to the end.
And when everything's over,
we'll arrive,
the latecomers,
a Soneira cart moaning
in the now deserted valley of Jehoshaphat.

Giuseppe Belli
Four Sonnets
Translated by Mike Stocks

In the early 1830s the poet Giuseppe Belli (1791–1863) unleashed an explosion of sonnets in the romanesco dialect of his native Rome, writing an incredible 1747 poems in the five years from 1831–5. Marinaded in a lifetime's exposure to the splendour and squalor of his city, and using the licence of dialect to purchase a subject matter and diction that no other European poets were dealing in, he resolved 'to leave a monument that shows the common people of Rome as they are today'. Figures from every course of life – housewives, mothers, beggars, lovers, businessmen, popes, idiots, whores, doctors, thieves, lawyers, priests, chancers, pen-pushers, bin-men, shop girls, actresses, grave-diggers, depressives, servants, sex-addicts, gossips and hundreds more – speak of themselves and each other in all the grubby beauty of their unfettered human preoccupations, and in a plain-speaking diction that Wordsworth and Coleridge in their preface to the *Lyrical Ballads* could hardly have imagined possible. The whole is like a *Canterbury Tales* or a *Decameron* of sonnets, rendering up a complete society.

The benchmark of Belli translations into English, or into

English dialects, or into sister languages such as Scots, is surely
the work of the Scots poets Robert Garioch and William Neill.
They are the only Belli translators to date who have attempted
(and achieved) the greatest balancing act of formal verse
translation: full metre, full rhyme, and a fidelity to the content
and spirit of the originals while achieving an independently
viable poetry in the translations.

(Mike Stock's own Belli will be published by Oneworld
Classics in June 2007. See also *MPT* 3/3 for some versions of
Belli by Paul Howard.)

Girl with scruples

Oh bloody hell, so not one kiss from you?
One little fondle in the bra you wear?
Don't worry, I'll be careful what I do,
I only want to feel what's under there...

You've scruples? And for what? We're family and
I might go fucking you . . . ?! Yeah right, oh please—
we're cousins' cousins, can't you understand?
If we're related, so are chalk and cheese!

Related . . . ! God, what namby-pambiness,
and all this bother for a kiss with you
when Father Charles, oh him, he gets a screw!

What's up, you think that Jesus could care less
if you get chatted up by me and kissed?
He doesn't even think of stuff like this.

La scrupolosa

Inzomma, cazzo, se pò avé sto bbascio?
se pò ttastà un tantino er pettabbotto?
Ma nnun avé ppavura, che ffo adascio:
cuanto che ssento che cce tienghi sotto.

Ciai scrupolo? e dde cosa? E cche! tte fotto?!
Semo parenti? Sí, ppe vvia der cascio:
cuggini de cuggini: cascio cotto:
parenti come Ggnacchera e ssan Biascio.

Parenti, ggià! cche scrupoli der tarlo!
Per un bascio co mmé ttanta cusscenza,
eppoi te fai fischià ddar Padre Carlo.

Ma cche ccredi? che Cristo abbi pascenza
d'abbadà ssi tte bbascio, o ssi tte parlo?
A ste cojjonerie manco sce penza.

What does he do, the Pope?

What does he do, the Pope? He fools around,
has sleepy-poos, drinks coffee, stuffs his face,
waves from the window, slobs around the place,
takes Rome to be his private stomping ground.

No brats for him – he couldn't give a toss
about a big supporting band of kids,
since even if the city hits the skids
there'll always be some soup left for the boss.

The water, air and sun, the bread and wine,
he thinks he owns the lot – *it's mine, all mine!* –
as if the whole shebang's a one-man show.

It's like the sly old dog would love to find
himself alone – as God was, years ago,
before He made the angels and mankind.

Cosa fa er Papa?

Cosa fa er Papa? Eh ttrinca, fa la nanna,
taffia, pijja er caffè, sta a la finestra,
se svaria, se scrapiccia, se scapestra,
e ttiè Rroma pe ccammera-locanna.

Lui, nun avenno fijji, nun z'affanna
a ddirigge e accordà bbene l'orchestra;
perché, a la peggio, l'úrtima minestra
sarà ssempre de quello che ccommanna.

Lui l'aria, l'acqua, er zole, er vino, er pane,
li crede robba sua: *È tutto mio*;
come a sto monno nun ce fussi un cane.

E cquasi quasi godería sto tomo
de restà ssolo, come stava Iddio
avanti de creà ll'angeli e ll'omo.

The pregnant mum

No kidding? Well praise be to God, Susanna,
you're really well and truly up the duff!
I hope the Holy Virgin and Saint Anna
protect you now – and when you do your stuff.

What month are you? Mm-hm, the ninth you say?
If bellies tell the truth, to look at it
it's not a girl, the nipper on its way,
though in the end you'll get what God deems fit.

And can you feel him kick, the little man?
Then walk a bit, get plenty food and drink,
and leave the rest to nature's ancient law . . .

None of your nonsense, now, come on, just think
– to chase away the terrors, if you can –
how many have been through this all this before.

La primaròla

E accusí? ggrazziaddio, sora Susanna,
l'avemo arzata poi la trippettona?
Che la bbeata Vergine e Ssant'Anna
ve protegghino, e ssia coll'ora bbona.

E in che lluna mó state? Ah, in de la nona.
Eh, ar véde, si la panza nun inganna,
pare che nun dev'èsse una pissciona,
ma ssarà arfine quer ch'Iddio ve manna.

Ve la sentite in corpo la cratura?
Dunque bboni bbocconi, e ccamminate;
e llassate fà er resto a la natura.

Ggnente: tutte ssciocchezze. Voi penzate,
pe llevàvve da torno la pavura
quante prima de voi sce sò ppassate.

A miraculous relic

This much I know: among the rare sensations
and relics that the Popes have gathered for
the prefect of the Sacristry to store
in holy shrines with the authentications,

Christ's foreskin – plus his other little bits
and vital members – is the pride and joy;
as relics go it's just the real McCoy,
and any other relic looks like shit

compared . . . Now then, my dear good sir, don't say
this holy foreskin also seems to hail
from other countries which lay claim to it;

have faith my man, have faith, a little bit.
There could be eighty foreskins? Fine, okay—
perhaps it grew and grew, like fingernails.

Un'erlíquia miracolosa

Questo io lo so cche ttra li pezzi rari
d'erliquie che li Papi hanno provisto
e ttiè in conzeggna Monziggnor Zagristo
coll'utentiche drento all'erliquiari,

sc'è er prepuzzio c'aveva Ggesucristo
coll'antri su' membrucci nescessari,
ch'è un erliquione che ssopra all'artari
pò ccacà in faccia ar mejjo che ss'è vvisto.

E nun zerve de dí, ccaro sor Muzzio,
che cc'è ppiú d'un paese che ss'avvanta
d'avé er tesoro der zanto prepuzzio.

Fede, sor Muzzio mio, fede bbisoggna.
Ebbè? mmagaraddio fussino ottanta?
Je sarà aricressciuto com'e ll'oggna.

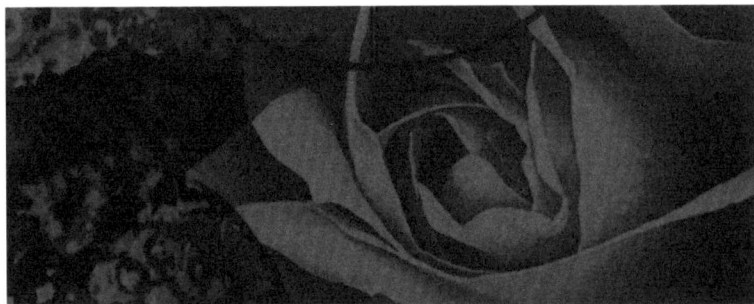

Elsa Morante
'Farewell'
An extract translated by Cristina Viti

Internationally renowned for her novels *La storia* (*History*) and *L'isola di Arturo* (*Arturo's Island*), Elsa Morante (1912–1985) was one of the most versatile writers of her time.

The natural daughter of a Jewish teacher who remained married to her children's official father, a tutor in a youth custody centre, Morante had no formal schooling until her teens. After completing her high school education, she left home and immediately began her writing career with contributions to various magazines.

1941–42 saw the publication of her first books: a collection of short stories, a translation of Katherine Mansfield's *Scrapbook* and a children's story with her own illustrations.

Having married writer Alberto Moravia, Morante followed him into hiding after he was accused of 'antifascist activities', and around that time began work on the novel *Menzogna e sortilegio* (*House of Liars*), which was to be her first huge success: the Premio Viareggio she was awarded in 1948 marked the beginning of thirty years of travels and intense engagement in intellectual debate, during which she added to her publishing credits more stories and novels, as well as several essays, regular

collaborations with several periodicals and a poetry collection,
Alibi.

In 1980, about two years before the publication of her last
novel, *Aracoeli*, Morante found her mobility and health severely
impaired by complications following a thighbone fracture,
and in 1983 she attempted suicide by gas. Rushed to hospital
by her maid and operated upon following a diagnosis of
hydrocephaly, she remained in the clinic until her death by
heart attack in November 1985.

Below is an excerpt from *Addio (Farewell)*, the opening section
of *Il mondo salvato dai ragazzini e altri poemi* (*The World Saved by
Kids and Other Epics*), a work Morante expressly commended to
young people, 'the only audience that might still be capable of
listening to the word of poets'. Hailed by Antonio Porta as
one of the most important works of the 1968–78 decade, the
book incorporates verse, drama, musical notation, handwriting,
layout alterations and other surprises to create a statement of
irreducible vitality. The current Einaudi edition bears on the
cover a painting by Bill Morrow, the young American artist
whose arrival in Rome in 1961 and tragic death in New York
a year later marked a turning-point in Morante's life.

I

    Day after day the howl of the morning
jolts me out of the moonless place of your silence.
O heavenly night without resurrection
forgive me if once again I return to these voices.

    I press my ear to the ground
to an absurd echo of the buried beats.
Behind the fleeing unattainable beast
I throw myself onto the scent of blood.

I want to save you from the slaughter that steals you
and take you back to sleep in your little bed.
But ashamed of your wounds you conceal
the pathways that lead to your lair.

I sham and laugh in a desperate dance
to distract you from the horrifying gloom
but your eyes discoloured under their eyelids
no longer wink at my love tricks.

Searching for your colours for your smile
I course the cities along a fading track.
Each boy that goes by is a mirage.
I think I recognize you, for a moment.

And begging I run after a flickering curl
or a red T-shirt flitting round a corner . . .
But holed up in your cold hideaway
you despise my pitiful comedy.

A useless fool I rave roaming the streets
where every living breath denies you.
Then, at sundown, upturn on the desolate threshold
a game-bag full of bloodied feathers.

And I ask of the room's darkness some tenderness,
at least some decaying of memory,
senility, the equivocation of vulgar time
that *heals all sorrows* . . .

But your death increases by the day.
And in this mounting spate I fall and rush back up
in a reckless race, for some sign,
some pointer in your direction.

O unattainable and beloved nest,
there is no earthly step leads me to you.
Perhaps outside of days and of places?
Your death is the voice of a siren.

Perhaps through some perdition? or some grace?
or in what poison? in what drug?
perhaps in reason? or perhaps in sleep?
Your death is the voice of a siren.

Lust for a sleep that feels like some sweetness from you
but was the very imposture where I lost you!
Your death is the voice of a siren
that would sidetrack me into her pits away from you.

Perhaps, I have to accept every field rule:
each single degradation, each single patience.
I cannot jump over this barbed wire fence
while your innocent cry goes unanswered.

Your death is a blinding light in the night
it is an obscene laugh in the morning sky.
I am sentenced to the time and to the places
until the scandal is consummated over me.

Right here, I have to scheme and bargain with the beast
to rob it of the secret of my treasure.
O restraint of a slain childhood,
forgive me this indecency of surviving.

II

You left thinking you were playing the runaway.
Trying for *Bravo!* with your farewell grimace.
Same old story! To then banish yourself to your cubbyhole
menacing behind your barred-up doors
like a great captain in his ultimate fort
– woe on the audacious one should dare a siege!
But I know you. If nobody will dare
you'll tear yourself apart, and weep in childish anger
because there's no love in the world and you're forsaken.

But this time, your door was slammed by hurricanes.
Rains rushed through the forlorn apartment
and a blood-like silt spattered the walls.
When you were alive, your room was the neighbourhood
   star,
sought after by all. And now
everyone shuns it, as if it were plague-ridden.
My foot stumbles on your poor vest
that no one's bothered to pick up from the floor. On the
   balcony
ravaged by winters, your plants have died.

Even thieves have sniffed at your ultimate fief
where indeed there was precious little to steal!
Cut out from magazines, the portraits of your heroes
still adorn the walls: Gautama the Sublime,
bearded Fidel, suicide Billie Holiday.
Your cat's bowl is still sitting in a corner.
A thin red necktie hangs in the closet.

You left saddling yourself with your main possessions:
the cat in her basket and the portable phonograph.
'The rest of the luggage, ship it to me by sea'.
Three hundred times that ship has crossed that sea
and your treasures lie scattered, and I am here, alive.
Should I live three thousand years, course every sea,
I can no longer reach you to bring you back.

I know you thought you were playing farewell.
It was bravado, that grimace of yours . . .
But against the impatient wager of a boy
the stake at play is another drawn-out agony.

  The thief of nights is a blind and deranged camel,
  she roams enchanted Saharas, outside all tracks.
  The route is lunatic, there is no destination.
  The sands undo the traces of her thieving.

  Her white eyes make mirages grow
  from the torn bodies she sows across the sands.
  And the mirages shift to multiplied distances
  unattainable within their lonely fields.

  Amputated off their bodies, they scatter, irredeemably
  separate, eternal mutilations.
  No mirage can meet another mirage.
  Only solitudes are left, after the theft of bodies.

  No addresses out there, nor any names, nor hours.
  No sign for mutual recognition. The whole eternal
     infinity
  is nothing but an empty white sky, sleepwalking wheel
  where one flees blindly absent from the other.

  The only chance to meet had been
  this poor terrestrial point.

....

And now here alone in this wake of ages
sitting in a corner of the room by the door
behind the window lit up in the night
I wait for the time of your return home.

I cannot give myself up to sleep, while you delay.
I want to have you back next to me, feel your breath
and cleanse you from the impossible leprosy
that has disfigured the mirth of your eyes.

I spy through the glass panes, listen out. In the distance
the bleak noise of the streets flows on like a toothed strip.
All the cities on earth are one goddamned gang in cahoots
against the heavenly kids.

The sleazy barflies, the malignant queens,
the ugly toxic rooms of cigarettes
the deafening basements
the demented homicidal fists
the cop chases
the traffics
the distorted signals
the gardens of vampires
the wards of hospitals in delirium
the film stars the dolls the fairies the ambassadors the
                                    middlemen the contracted killers
the little baroque palazzos the skyscrapers
the urinals
the slimy stairs of bridges the river shacks
and the railway tracks . . .
Latest Evening News
'With a blood-curdling scream'.

Without respite I pace from door to window.
I listen out with every step in the street.
And the long night advances. The rustle of wheels along the
    tarmacs
grows less frequent. The shop signs go out.

The last lit-up windows are shut.
No more steps on the pavements.
No more gates screeching. An end to every late shudder
of the lift with its hoarse cogs past all floors.

Until in the fading of the silent hour
a slumber bends my eyelids. My forehead crashes
down on the tabletop almost slamming
among my dishevelled white hair.

        And so, like in love endings . . .

And so I didn't hear your step, nor the clinking
of the little bunch of keys, nor the door opening
as you come home. Two childish hands
are tickling my nape.

I recognize, near my face, the nestlike flavour
of your hair. With my uncertain gaze I make out
the luminous shadows of your eyes, the colour of a
    star-studded sea.
'You hoodlum – is this the time? Here you are at last!

You might have told me, last night, you'd be out for the
    night!
What've you been up to? Something happen to you? some
    fight? who crossed you?
Or some sickness . . . they got you drinking – again! did
    you fall over? . . .
did you get hurt? where does it hurt?' . . .

'I am not hurt. I'm not in any pain.
Look at me, I'm well. Look, my body is intact.
But you – how old you've grown! you've gone and shrunk on
    me!
Your hair's all white! your *lashes* are white!

When you smile, your face puckers up even more!
Poor cute funny little old lady.
I've come to say good-night.
This is the hour of healing.

The hideous ferocious sickness that undermined us both
ends here. For all of my cruelties
I ask your forgiveness. And likewise I forgive you your
cruelty.

You knew that earthly childhoods
are a passage of divine barbarians
bearing the jailhouse mark of the ordained end.
You knew that. And yet you'd have me live
when I would live no longer.
Your prevarication was a hassle for me.

The old, if they rejoice in a kid's presence,
see nothing in him but mirth. See nothing else.
You worshipped as a feast of your destiny
a marked childhood that spoke its sickness to you.

Mirthful with the childhood I brought to you
you forgot the monotonous law that embroiders
its spectral patterns with an automaton's hand.
Your carefree ways were an insult to me.

Denying the nature that sentenced me from the start,
you would not understand me! To save
your only happiness and gratitude
you waved your fibs around like amulets.

When the spirits of slaughter threw me down with a howl
you stroked me where I'd fallen and said it was nothing.
When my conscious eyes full of fear
asked you for help, you kissed them, laughing.

You distracted me from insomnia with your fables
and listened to my dreams' desperate prophecies as if
they were fairy tales. You promised me I'd become
a king on earth, while earth was banishing me.

But I knew I was a cornered bandit.
To leave the game as a winner, laughing in the hangman's
    face,
I had nothing but another violence: my own, and precocious,
free with the last hooray! – and you fought me for it.

And so, through the meanness of your happiness,
you shopped me to the obtuse slaughter police
for the routine degradation procedure:
jailhouse, ugliness, decay.

And then, perhaps, once I was ugly, ruined, you too would
    have banished me.
You are too childish! and mad! I know you!
I have always known you. That's why I am smiling at you
and have come to say good-bye. You are all my heart.

Even if I'm a mirage
don't be afraid of the daylight that might steal me from you.
Tonight, very soon, you too will be made a mirage.
The day has no more time to surprise you.

Even if my name is delirium,
rest in this smile of my good-night.
Only at this ultimate point could you still meet me.
This is our farewell'.

  The thief of nights is a demented maniac
  she hides each theft always in a different hole.
  There is never a way out of those segregations.
  There is no corridor or courtyard for those endless
      houses of reclusion.
  No common wall between one cell and the next.

  The fantastic distance separating them
  brooks no measure. No message is possible.
  The rooms doorless: no windows, no top vents.
  No post or alphabets or telephones or cipher books.

  No pass you can cross through those ruinous
  hungering dunes. No body of water for ships.
  No body of air for voices.

  But when memory is chewed up by the sands
  even the pulse of grief is cut short.

  So be it.

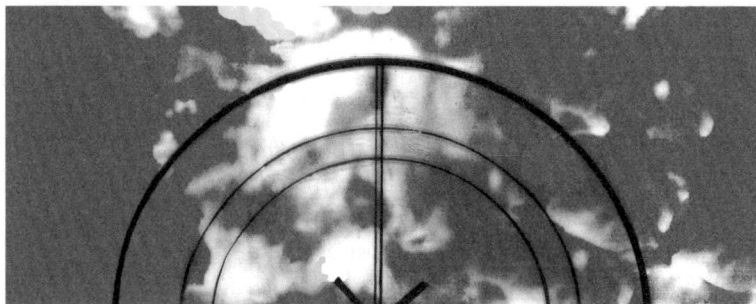

Andrea Zanzotto
Four poems
Translated by Jo Catling and others

In-Coherence: Under the Influence of Andrea Zanzotto

Three years after the appearance of *La Beltà* in 1968, Pier Paolo Pasolini wrote in an unfinished essay that in the poetry of Andrea Zanzotto the 'semantic field' becomes limitless; in fact the poem itself becomes limitless, or so we can infer. 'One never knows in which semantic field one is situated: the reader is drawn into an unprecedented condition of estrangement from that to which he is accustomed.' But it is not only the semantic field, or the subject of Zanzotto's poetry, which is puzzling; puzzling too is what that 'one' is and what that 'being situated' is. 'One is situated': many of Zanzotto's poems seem to be saying that 'none' ('not-me', 'nought-us', 'July-I') is situated, that a 'none' exists, a condition without categories. Readers of this poetry may feel that no one is situated in the poem, that 'one' in fact is dying and that in this death another space opens. The poems of Andrea Zanzotto seem to be full of the dead. And the dead are silently expressive. The poems speak from a non-point-of-view: 'Ah, and None'.

Not speaking through the authority of an I, not speaking subjectively, the poems however seem to be part of a process of joining up again with the world, merging word and world; they merge with the world almost as the dead have merged by losing their authority and power. A new authority speaks in this poetry, a new eminence or pre-eminence which is low down, 'un'altezza nuova', a new height which is that of the dead and that of the insects, the rabbits, the small birds on low branches and of the blades of grass and stalks of hay. There is a tiny elevation in the poems, about as high as a grasshopper jumps. The poems are microscopic, which means they do not magnify, they microfy and microspy. They do not look through eyes and needle-eyes, they know of even tinier openings into the 'other'. They distinguish by extinguishing; there is a quenching going on and a dwindling. In the birdsong poem printed here – 'Under the Influence' – the interest lies with the minimality of the sounds produced by the birds: their singing is not a signifying, it is a 'sig-sig-signifying', something between a 'sic' and a 'sigh', a burst of breath and an intimate expression of sadness.

Over a period of six months, 'i Zanzottini' met weekly, sometimes twice-weekly for ever longer and more intensive sessions, in a combination of translation workshop and research seminar, discussing the poems, the sounds, the intertextual resonances and – most of all – the in-between spaces: interstices, *crune* and lacunae. Like rabbit-holes, or mirrors, these are sites of dis/orientation where 'meaning' emerges and through which it escapes, enacting the passing or transgressing into an altered state – a metaphor for both poem and translation. The translations can be seen as after-images of this process, reflecting not only Zanzotto's work but also resonating with our own various intellectual and poetic preoccupations, as well as our other languages: Italian, German, French, Spanish, Norwegian and Portuguese. Dante – and Hölderlin – have been constant companions on the journey through the often dark wood of Zanzotto's verse; and echoes, after-images of

Rilke and Celan, Hopkins and Lewis Carroll, Venice and the Veneto have all left their traces. The poems offered here are both product and by-product, after-images of the Zanzotto poems and the struggle to preserve their elusiveness.

Andrea Zanzotto was born in 1921 in the small town of Pieve di Soligo in the province of Treviso, a few miles north of Venice, and he has always lived there. During the Second World War he was a messenger for the Resistenza movement. He studied literature at the Università di Padova and became a secondary school teacher. Since *Dietro il paesaggio* (1951), twelve books of poems have appeared; Zanzotto is also the author of a book of prose, *Sull'Altopiano*, and of two books of critical writings, *Fantasie di avvicinamento* (1991) and *Aure e Disincanti nel novecento letterario* (1994).

'I Zanzottini' are: Will Buck, Jo Catling, Megan Clark, Aaron Deveson, Jonathan Evans, Eugenia Loffredo, Stefan Tobler, Peter Waterhouse.

We are grateful to the Leverhulme Trust for sponsoring Peter Waterhouse as Leverhulme Visiting Professor at the University of East Anglia.

More Zanzotto, translated by Peter Hainsworth, in *MPT* 3/6, 'After Images'.

So We Are

They would say, in Padova, 'me too',
the friends, 'I knew him.'
And there was the pounding of foul water
nearby, and of a foul workshop:
magnificent in the silence.
It being night. 'Me too
I knew him.'
Vividly I thought
of you who now
are neither subject nor object
neither common speech nor jargon
neither still nor movement
not even the nor that negated
and no matter how deeply
my eyes enter its needle-eye
never negates you enough.

And so be it: but I
believe with equal
passion in all my nothingness,
therefore I have not lost you
or, the more I lose you and the more you lose you
the more you are like me, the closer you come.

Under the Influence

Birds
raw infinite chirping
on a wintry tree
some thing raw
perhaps not true but single
spark of a maybe
infantly a-human
but certainly here with us listening
         – alarmed – distant
         – or even calmed – distant
birds an entire city
pregnant   enclosed
                 glottal glories
                 treacherous teachings
an enclosed sig-sig-signifying
not even infant but
adult occult in its minimity

               [dispersed species of my sleep
               that will never return]

There Was Someone

As one evening we arrived
between clouds and grass   a bit scattered   off
the she and two little ones and sweet excited shadows . . .
Wood ferment   surplus of smell
and that I-was purely physical
and I was standing in poorest July:
      undisturbed, July-I, by me and by mine
I not undisturbed, all of them (so sudden) bunnies.
Because it was there: so locked so tiny
so lost, the small stall. And dreamed by a sober dream
by the non-enthusiastic gaze – the grass
right up to the window-sills –
the rabbits mother and sons in the small stall
a bit prisoners a bit   Ah, and
I don't love them I am not them and none is them.   None.
And everything is almost without colours, they look at it,
hay stalk by stalk they tooth and look: if it's raining?
Lasting in rabbit-wood the evening
here, two stalks nibbled at, the eye
bit sweet a bit scared.
And what story far far away.
Knowing that it's not a walk.
Purity (the least) peeping open, only two steps, and very
   beyond,
in other words we: were there a link between us
were there a liking for a bit of food
were we, in the brightness of the evening . . .
Mummy-rabbit two young ones and – bead by bead –
in the scattered, stray.   Out of focus
But finally all is not nothing
if all soft softly rabbits weightless
co-rabbitation. And I draw no more

than sticks in the evening, than the curtain of rain,
than hay entangled between signs   and I heard:
hinny yowl hum   on the reverse in the plication.
Once there was someone, now
nibbling, twitching where there's a chance.
A perfected sign-design
anyway: from here it will bolt:
to enrabbit us to make us
clamber, long limbs, climbing, going where
            – The teacher says so
            so says Lewis and Alice.

Outrange Outrage	Tragedy Outrage

You hop grasshop frictive
  pure-pre
into the void   spin into   out
you do away with yourself
out of touch – all in all –
all in all
all
you are away
I see you in the depths of my
  closedarknight
I distinguish you between the
  nons the sics the sighs
I extinguish you
no one yes one one
full of spines heartless freezing
you do away with yourself
and plunge and undo yourself
  into yourself evermore into
  yourself
out the camp
avoid away
plunge into your
you blinding violent seamless
  nil
the exploding the energy and it
  can't be heard
nothing to be heard
no   you hopped far away
opulent grasshopping away
	You hop grasshop sizzling pure
	  man-woman
	into the void push outré
	you push in further
	intangibly – in conclusion –
	in conclusion
	in
	you are further in there
	I see you in the depths of my
	  darkclosednight
	I identify you by the nose the
	  sight the sighs
	I disidentify you
	one no one yes one
	cruel cold full of nails
	you push in further
	and founder and too far in you
	  always further in you
	fuck the whole field
	face death
	in your founder
	sparkling ferocious unseamless
	  nothing
	exploding shattering and not
	  feeling
	nothing not feeling
	no you are dropped further in
	  there
	rich grasshopping there

The out-rage	The outrage

Insult Outsult   Oltranza Oltraggio

Hop grasshop frittering   Salti saltabecchi friggendo
    pure-inpure   puro-pura
out   thrust   through   nel vuoto   spinto   outré
you make for   ti fai più in là
untouchable – together –   intangibile – tutto sommato –
to gather   tutto sommato
gathered   tutto
you are far more   sei più in là
I see you deep in my   ti vedo nel fondo della mia
    cameraoscura   serachiusascura
identify you twixt hic and sic and   ti identifico tra i non i sic i
    sigh   sigh
inidentify you   ti disidentifico
only no only yes all alone   solo no solo sì solo
full of prickles stinging frigid   piena di punte immite frigida
you make for   ti fai più in là
you profounder and too far in you   e sprofondi e strafai in te
    always further in you   sempre più in te
frig off the field   fotti il campo
die verse   decedi verso
yourwards profounder   nel tuo sprofondi
you pulse fierce seamless   brilli feroce inconsutile
    inexistent   nonnulla
the bursting the blatant and   l'esplodente l'eclatante e non si
    nothing feeling   sente
nothing feels nothing   nulla non si sente
no   you've hopped over there   no   sei saltata più in là
happy go hopping   there   ricca saltabeccante   là

The result   L'oltraggio

Author's Note

Oltranza Oltraggio (Outrage Outrage)

Oltranza oltraggio: in the sense of 'thing that goes beyond the limit, what is bearable' ('e cede la memoria a tanto oltraggio' [and memory fails at such outrage] cf. Dante, *Paradiso*, XXXIII, 57). *Sigh*: this is the well-known English sigh-hiccup used in comics. *Fotti il campo*: a non-translation, half sense and half non-sense from the French 'foutre le camp', to scarper.

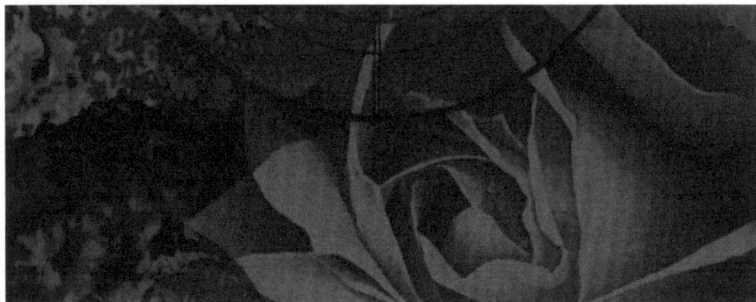

Elena Shvarts
Nine Poems
Translated by Sasha Dugdale

Elena Shvarts is one of Russia's greatest living poets. These
poems here are from a new collection of her work in my
translation, *Birdsong on the Seabed* , to be published by Bloodaxe
early 2008.

Shvarts stands outside all schools and movements in con-
temporary Russian poetry. She once famously described poetry
as a 'dance without legs'. Her own poetry fits this description
perfectly, a combination of deeply rhythmic and lyrical dance
with eccentric, perpetual movement of flight.

The world of her poems is strange and grotesque; often the
setting is urban, but unrecognisable – towns emptied of the
everyday and peopled only by animals, spirits and strange
elemental forces. A peculiar religious fervour illuminates these
scenes, but her religion is unorthodox and highly individual.

Shvarts' poetry is visionary. Her vision takes her to the edge
of language and rhythm, and she is one of the few poets alive
who is brave enough to trust her vision absolutely.

Elena Shvarts is a poet and prose writer. Born in St
Petersburg in 1948, she studied at the Leningrad Institute of
Film, Music and Theatre. The daughter of a theatre literary

manager, she earned her living translating plays for
Leningrad's theatres. Her poems were published in samizdat
and abroad from the late 60s, but her first Russian publication,
Circle, did not appear until 1984. Since then she has published
more than ten collections of poetry. A book of prose pieces,
including short autobiographical fragments, *The Visible Side of
Life*, was published in 2003. She was awarded the Andrei Bely
Literary Prize in 1979, and the Triumph Prize in 2003, an
independent award for a lifetime's achievement in the arts.

Betrothal to Fontanka

To you, despicable river
I am betrothed, like the Doge
Throwing that ring to the water's depths,
And I am the body of my beloved cat
Who slept by me, slumbered
So many years,
Purred, sung a guttural song . . .
In her eyes love
Lit two tiny candles,
When she (as always) followed me.
The river lay like a hand
In the dissecting room
And the ray of a heavenly lancet
Cuts bare the blue sinew,
Here lessons in the soul's
Anatomy, here my Rembrandt . . .
You waste-laden, vicious, naked thing

You barely stir the water-weed,
Now it's you – forever at my side,
Never taking your dim, deepwater eyes off me
Staring with your sand
And fish and leeches and slippery creatures –
You bid them all talk with me.

Above the gulf's fingers . . .

Above the gulf's fingers, the plains and the flatlands
The peaks and the troughs and the depths
Eyes take wing, sight ascend
As if I had cast you myself.
Fly above water, rising and falling,
Fly, and if you can't, slide,
And let me forget in the effort of gliding
My self and my own fretted life.

Land of destruction, ancient Strelna,
Leech-placid you cling
Under the arm and close to the heart
Of a bitter city-edge spring.

My eyes have wings, my sight ascends
Through waves, high places, beyond.
See that cloud over there? And the rainbow – look!
And if you can't find me, when you turn back –
Fly over the sea and on.

Why not everyone sees angels

Angels pass so very quickly
The eye can barely keep up
A moment's blaze rips day's cloth
Darkness runs to sew it up.

Eternity is short. Like a shadow
A golden flash briefly passed
I follow. My eye's palms clapping
Clapping. Got it. Mine, at last!

And if you stand quite still and turn
On needle tips
Eternity's golden disc revolves –
Her price – a wing lifts.

And if an angel of the apes
Should rest on your shoulder bone
There is no shoulder and no sorrow
No angel. Candlelight alone.

The Bear's Dream

I won't have strange forces write me
Like a slate.
I won't whistle to the humbled tune
Of fate.

I meet every new day with blessed
Happiness
Sweet comfort, this cup of tea,
My idleness.

A blessing too, that you are loved
By none
Your closest lie with withered lips
In tombs.

And on we fly – round, sharp
Shot from a gun
Brothers, sisters, dissolve, vanish
Husbands gone.

And all of it, boot to hat –
Coat-stuffing
Becomes dust suspended
Merciful nothing

But who rests a paw on my shoulders,
Lifts himself?
In me, in this wild den,
A bear dwells.

All life is winter, and in winter
He shrinks in size and moans
But the moment comes and he wears
You into the world, breaking bones

And now in spring – yes, spring –
The singing thaw
Darting looks – he is with me –
And we shall roar.

The Freeing of Fox

Through the dead silver glint of valley
Over the firm snow
Over stiff-frozen flakes
Runs fox
On three paws.
The crumpled fourth lies
Bloodied in a trap.
Fox runs towards the shining summit
Now falling, now picking herself up again
Now a seething one-legged teenager
Now once more a beast in pain
On trembling paws.
There, at the summit, and waiting, her freedom
Heavenly Petersburg,
Familiar faces.
Fox runs, staining the clean snow
Howling gently
At the icy heavens.

The little girl and the rat

A girl walked out with a rat one day –
The rat sat splayed like a shoulder piece.
No one was the least bit surprised
Because this is the most ancient of dreams.
The rat darted looks, this way and that
The girl stroked the rat's hanging root
She herself greyer than an earthed-up tuber
Still without sproutings, buds or shoots
The snow covers them with its own grey fluff,
This most ancient of unions bemuses
The rat, blowing in the ear's thin cup –
(But in vain) – like an wordless Muse.

Birdsong on the Seabed

These days I am so very sad
Sad to the point of yawning –
Drowning down in dream.
Whirlpools softly spinning,
Oh, give in to the sea
To the moon, the water, the grief
Circling, I am falling
To the algae-blanketed seam
The muffled war-like ring
Of bells draped in weed.

Bird slides under the waves
Bends them by force of its wings

Amongst the glowing of stones
The ear-lobate curling
The waxy husk of shells
And the weed-serpent unfurling
Triton is swimming through,
Bird takes pains to hide
Wing-shovelling down
No nest-building on stone
Fish, no life amongst you,

But singing to the bed, to the boulder
In a watery Sodom-night
To the deafest fish of the deep
About the stars above streams,
The ancient skin of the oak,
About candlelight.

And about fire and brimstone
The *lampada*'s unending flame,
About the dust of moths
And brief moth-pain
And scorched moth-bone.

Bird slides under the waves
Bends them by force of its wings.

The bruise-blue salt corrodes the eye
Pain pecks at the beak.
Sing, perched on the bony arm
Of a drowned man, sing
Of his life's path, a candle he once lit.

Bird slides under the waves
Bends them by force of its wings.

Bird sings as if from the branch at dusk:
The shining garden, the sun
But the cold-blooded beasts believe
None of the tales of heat, none
But the shadowy seahorse believe –
When silent, willow o wisp
In the little round boat of a nutshell
Falls to the depths of the sea,
Then the sea-foal believes.

Is it worth singing where no one can hear,
Unrolling trills on the bed?
I am waiting for you, I lean from the boat –
Bird, ascend to the depths.

Candle at a Wake

I love fire so
That I kiss it,
Reach out towards it
Wash my face in it,
Since the gentle spirits
Inhabit it, like a bud,
And a band of magic
Thinly rings it.
This is their home, you see,
Their shell, their comfort,
And everything else
Is too earthy for them.

I set my fringe alight,
I singed my eyebrows,
I thought . . . it was you
Flickering there in the flame.
Perhaps you wanted
To whisper a word of light,
The flame quivers,
But I am filled with dark.

Cat presses close . . .

Cat presses close, as if she were sleeping
And murmurs a whiskery song,
And listens to my heart racing,
My time rushing on.
The earth turns, as it's used to turn,
Like a truck, on a prayer and a dime
The grass waking under a skin,
Yet sleep – the sun arcs again,
Sleep – how much has the blood left to course
In these sheltering cones of flesh,
As much as snow, still to slip through the glass –
And that knows the wintering bear, and one's breath.

Reviews and Comments

Michael Hamburger
Perplexities about Assia Wevill
A note on *A Lover of Unreason*, by Yehuda Koren and
Eilat Negev
Robson Books 2006
ISBN 1861059744
Hb. £20

Having long since ceased to be a book reviewer, least of all of revelations about the private lives of persons known to me as writers or as friends, I had a special reason for making an exception of *A Lover of Unreason: The Life and Death of Assia Wevill*. It was that I had two connections with her, both of which had become blanks in my mind. The first was that I was persuaded to write an Introduction to the early book of *Selected Poems* by Yehuda Amichai which included a set of translations by Assia, though I felt incompetent to do so because, as I wrote in it, 'poems are made of words, and I cannot read the words of which Amichai's poems are made, cannot follow – let alone judge – his way with the Hebrew language, what he does with its ancient and modern, literary and vernacular components . . .' I hoped to discover from this biography who persuaded me – Ted Hughes, his sister Olwyn, the editor at Penguin or Assia herself; also what part Ted Hughes had in these translations. If there was correspondence in the matter, I have lost or mislaid it. I also failed to receive copies of the first printing, by Cape Goliard, of these versions, and of the second printing of them in the USA. It is my friend Oliver Bernard who tells me now that my Introduction was included in the American edition. All I have is the Penguin paperback of 1971, published after Assia's death, in which my Introduction is copyrighted with the date 1968, before Assia's death. In the Penguin edition the translations by Assia and those by Harold Schimmel are described as done 'with the collaboration of Ted Hughes'. What I know is that Ted Hughes continued to translate Amichai with various collaborators up to the time of his death, and I have a copy of his Amichai translation *Amen* (Harper USA, 1977) with his inscription. No light at all is cast on these perplexities by *A Lover of Unreason*; but, to me, those Amichai versions of Assia's are among the very little that remains of her life and work, since she took even her small daughter with her into death.

The second connection was a single longish meeting with Assia which I could neither date nor locate. It belonged to a phase in which both my family life and professional life were under such pressure that nothing could sink in, nothing be recorded or registered in memory. Again, the biographical book did not fill the gap. It was only by searching through a collection of old pocket diaries, after reading the book, that I found the date of the meeting – 3 January 1969, only weeks and days before Assia's death. That no surname, address, telephone number or time of day followed the name 'Assia' in that diary entry suggests that we must have been in touch earlier on – perhaps about the Amichai versions? The meeting, in any case, must have been at Assia's house in Clapham.

Insecurity was at the root of Assia's troubles throughout her life; and the causes of that insecurity are fully documented in this biography. At the moment of our only longer meeting, though, I too was beset by insecurity, all the continuities of my life being in suspense. As well as being preoccupied, most probably I did not know Assia well enough to have sensed just how close she was to her ultimate crisis point. What is more, I was about to leave London for a semester's teaching in the USA. So the question for me remains how much of Assia's desperation transpired in the long conversation we had then; but I have no recollection whatever of what we talked about, why she invited me to her flat or whether she told me enough to have made that meeting a call for the intervention I might at least have attempted, as a friend of Ted Hughes. The only thing that has stayed with me of that meeting is an illuminated script she showed me of poems by Ted Hughes with her art work – another collaboration, another of those labours of love, not copy-writing, which ought to have out-lasted her and may or may not be lost; and something tells me still that it is by this script that she wished me to remember her. The script is mentioned in passing by the biographers – because I recalled it when approached by them – but its preservation or destruction is left in doubt.

Of the biography I will say only that Yehuda Koren and Eilat Negev have done all they could to trace the facts and circumstances of Assia Gutmann's (then Wevill's) extra-ordinarily fragmented life, from antecedents Ukrainian and Latvian-Jewish on her father's side, German and Christian on her mother's, to Berlin, Palestine, South Africa, Canada and England; her three marriages, her employments in advertising agencies and associations with poets more or less famous. Her beauty, charm and accomplishments are copiously attested. So are her mainly frustrated erotic and sexual associations, down to the successive abortions and the final one of herself and her only child, when she was 41. So much emphasis falls on Ted Hughes, Sylvia Plath and David Wevill – whom I was not to meet till later, in 1974 – that the book did remind me of another meeting, my only longer conversation with Sylvia Plath soon before *her* death, at the PEN Anthology party in October 1962. There I had been struck by *her* hectic desperation, but was unable, of course, to meddle in affairs that were not my business.

Most of the reports from which the book is drawn are necessarily retrospective, with only brief extracts from Assia's own diaries and letters. This makes the book a contribution to the gossip, sensationalism and scandal-mongering that have become the price to be paid for celebrity; and, gifted though she was, Assia emerges as the victim of her self-doubts, self-estrangements and self-dramatizations, as a tragic catalyst in the arts – except for the few works that have qualified her as a subject in her own right, but the subject of a different kind of book.

Robin Fulton
Robertson's 'Afters'
A Note on Robin Robertson's 'versions' of
Tomas Tranströmer

Even a brief perusal of Lennart Karlström's substantial two-volume Tranströmer bibliography will give the impression that translating Tranströmer into English has become quite an industry in its own right. I suppose that, in terms of quantity, Robert Bly and myself have been most industrious: I like to think that Bly's American-English versions and my British-English versions complement each other nicely. Good-sized selections of his work have been published by, among others, Samuel Charters, Don Coles. John F Deane, Eric Sellin, and May Swenson (with Leif Sjöberg). At least half a dozen others have given us smaller selections. (Since there are so many gifted poetry-translators around, who can work directly from Swedish, might they not make an effort to bring some international recognition to some other Swedish poets who deserve such recognition but so far have not received much?)

Robin Robertson has now joined in, with 'new' versions
described by his publisher (Stephen Stuart-Smith, of the
notable Enitharmon Press) as 'gentle deviations rather than
literal translations'; and by Dr Karin Altenberg, Cultural
Affairs Officer of the Embassy of Sweden in London, as a 'fresh,
attentive' approach that has 'delighted' the poet. In publicity
material for Poetry International, London, October 2006,
Robertson describes the English texts by Bly and myself as
'literal translations'. I'm not sure what he means. I would say
that a translation is 'literal' if it simply lifts the word-order,
vocabulary, grammar and idioms of one language directly into
another without regard to what sort of sense or nonsense
results. At the very least, I would think that Bly's versions and
mine are in, shall we say, reasonably idiomatic English.

In the *Guardian* (28.10.06) Robertson tells us that the
Tranströmers have approved his English versions, and gives his
aim as steering a middle-ground 'between Lowell's rangy,
risk-taking rewritings and the traditional, strictly literal
approach'. (Wouldn't most translators of poetry say something
like that?) He also says he has 'opened out the sense of the
poem more clearly'. (As if the poet hadn't managed to make
clear what he wanted to?) What exactly is meant by
Transtömer's 'approval' or 'blessing' is not clear. Before his
stroke, in 1990, Transtömer's knowledge of both English and
German was good, and he has always kept an open and
unrestrictive attitude towards translations of his work, an
attitude which could perhaps be misused. Has Transtömer
been able to examine Robertson's versions in detail, or did he
simply give a friendly wave? It should be added here that the
idea of an 'imitation' is foreign to most Swedish poetry readers.

Before their publication as a small book, Robertson's
versions appeared in various magazines, presented as if they
were his own original poems. The contents list of *The London
Review of Books* (May 25, 2006) showed:

Page 25, Robin Robertson: Poem: 'Out in the Open'

and Robertson is listed among the contributors. On p. 25 we find 'after Tranströmer' in small print beneath the title: what we then read is not a 'version' or adaptation but a straight-forward line by line translation. Obviously, the poem should have been credited to its real author. (About a third of the text is identical to my translation, and there are several phrases identical to Bly's.)

In the June 2006 issue of *Poetry (Chicago)* we find Robertson's (sic) 'Homewards'. In the October issue, in a letter to the editor, Julia Shipley points out that my version and Robertson's are so similar that the latter 'seems simply an inferior translation, so what was the point of printing it?' In a haughty response, Robertson tells Shipley that she 'has not grasped the difference between a translation and a version', and claims that his version 'takes a number of liberties with the original but is, he hopes, 'an independent poem that is true to the tone of the Swedish'. Considering how arbitrary the few liberties are, and how the 'tone' is scarcely to be distinguished from that of many other translators of Tranströmer, it is hard to see how this particular translation, or any other of the same kind, can be regarded as an 'original poem'.

Robertson thanks Karin Altenberg 'for her invaluable help with the original texts'. In view of the 'liberties', either Robertson's knowledge of Swedish is very shaky, or he has ignored the advice of a native speaker. Altenberg must also, in view of her position in the Swedish Embassy, have helped in the promotion of the book: it was presented at Poetry International in London in October 2006, as a belated celebration of Tranströmer's 75th birthday. There was a repeat performance in Stockholm a month later; it was no doubt in connection with the latter that Robertson's winning of the major Forward Prize for 2006 was reported in the Swedish press – not exactly normal fare for Swedish newspaper readers. On the copyright page of the Enitharmon book Robertson's 'versions' are referred to as 'translations' and The Swedish Institute is thanked 'as sponsor of the translation costs'.

A few samples of 'liberties' ought to be given here. In 'Autumnal Archipelago' an elk is given 'hardwood' antlers, which it didn't have before, and a tree acquires the adjective 'horned'. In 'The Couple', 'the most secret thoughts' are turned into 'dreams'. My version of the last line is: 'a crowd whose faces have no expressions.' Bly's is: 'a mob of people with blank faces.' Robertson's: 'this audience of cancelled faces.' Why audience'? Why cancelled? In 'A Winter Night' (about half of which is identical to my translation) 'The storm has childish hands and wings' becomes 'The storm has the hands and wings of a child', and 'The Caravan bolts towards Lapland' (referring to the constellation) becomes 'Far away, travellers run for cover.' In 'Winter's Code' V, a metaphor is made into a simile and a spruce becomes a pine. In 'Out in the Open' (II) the Swedish verb 'myllrar' (swarm), referring to many things, becomes 'swell,' referring to one thing. And a few lines down, trees lose their tops. About 60% of 'To Friends behind a Frontier' is identical to my translation, but that still leaves space for a couple of 'liberties'.

In 'Sketch in October' (at least half of which is identical to my translation) we find an adjective wandering off to the wrong noun. And here, in 1.3, I have just spotted a slip which has lain unnoticed by sharp eyes for about two decades! The line ought to read: 'As if some people wanted to be fetched.' I wrote 'someone,' which was wrong. With their combined wits Altenberg and Robertson might have put me right here, but they didn't: they simply copied my mistake. In 'Calling Home' Robertson adds a grotesque line which has nothing whatsoever to do with what Tranströmer wrote. And in the final line where Tranströmer says 'I was like the needle in a compass . . .' we are given 'I dreamt I was the needle in a compass . . .' Some of Tranströmer's later poems are in a language so pared down, so free of rhetorical devices, that it is hard to see the possibility of different ways of translating them: they seem capable of slipping into almost any language. 'Midwinter' is an example:

Fulton:	Robertson:
A blue sheen	A blue light
radiates from my clothes,	streams out of my clothes.
Midwinter.	Midwinter.
Jangling tambourines	Ringing tambourines
of ice.	of ice.
I close my eyes.	I close my eyes.
There is a soundless world	There is a silent world,
there is a crack	there is a crack
where dead people	where the dead
are smuggled across the	are smuggled over the
border.	border.

'Light' is rather general for 'sken,' but is there anything much to choose between these versions? What is so 'new' about Robertson's?

When is a translation a translation and when is it a version? There is a wide sense in which every time we write or translate a poem we are, unwittingly or not, in touch with a labyrinth of previous poems and translations. This labyrinth is like the mycelium of a fungus, forming symbiotic relationships between fungi and the roots of plants: a system like this can spread over a large area of forest floor, enabling trees to communicate with and benefit from each other. There is another labyrinth, one in which poets deliberately imitate and adapt the work of others and present the result, or expect the result to be perceived, as somehow their own creation.

I have felt sceptical about this process ever since I made a youthful experiment about forty years ago. I wrote some imitations of four Italian poets and was surprised when Alan Ross published them (in 1966): I was not surprised when a gentleman from the Italian Embassy accused me of blasphemously interfering with the sacred texts of the poets. I thought he was pompous but I knew he had a point and I wished the book undone. (The fact that various people whose knowledge of Italian poetry and of the Italian language is better than mine seemed to like the book has not changed my mind.)

Lowell's name always crops up in such discussions. I can't help seeing the Lowell of *Imitations* as a colonial figure marching about the work of European poets, kicking things around in his search for something he can use. In 1968 I published an article in *Agenda* in which I tried to show how destructive Lowell's 'You Knocked Yourself Out' is of Ungaretti's 'Tu ti spezzasti.' Where Ungaretti is subtle, Lowell is brazen, as if lute music had been arranged for trombones. My plan was to write a second article, showing positively what Lowell had created out of Ungaretti, but I failed to find enough positive things to fill an article. That probably makes me an inadequate Lowell reader but I confess to having failed to find much good sense in his introduction to *Imitations*, in spite of having read it at regular intervals over the past forty-odd years. One thing is clear, though: Lowell set about trying to imagine or re-imagine a whole poem from the root upwards, creating a text which to his mind would stand relatively free of the original. Whether or not we care for the results we are dealing with something more thorough-going than simply changing a word here and there.

'Versions' of the Famous Dead have become popular in recent years. We have even seen an *Inferno*, hailed by the publisher as a translation that will restore the reader's faith in translation, but whose 'translator' admits in his own introduction that he can't make out much of what Dante actually wrote! The problem for the reader with works in this genre is that one never knows who is who. How much is Ovid, how much is Hughes? One can find out only by making a laborious comparison, and the results may not endear one to Hughes. My own slightly grumpy conclusion is: if you have a poem to write, write it, and if you don't, don't. Messing around with someone else's poem is no substitute.

In this wider context, Robertson's 'versions' can't in any way

be regarded as adaptations or imitations, let alone as
'independent poems'. His 'liberties' are local and arbitrary and
read like the flaws in an inept translation. Considering that
four of his fifteen versions are between a quarter and a third
identical to mine, and that no fewer than nine are a half or
more identical to mine, I'm not sure if he can call them 'his' at
all. In sum I think he has done a disservice to a fine poet.

Orpheus, don't come here

Tatiana Voltskaia
Cicada: Selected Poetry and Prose
Translated by Emily Lygo
Bloodaxe Books
ISBN: 1852247045
pb. £8.95

Tatiana Voltskaia came of age as a poet just as the Soviet
Union was disintegrating. Her first collections of poetry were
published in the late 1980s. At the same time she became
a journalist and essayist, working in various places, but
particularly associated with Radio Liberty. Voltskaia belongs
to the strange generation in the middle: She has neither the
long and dramatic career of a dissident, defined by hardship
and mythical standing, nor does she belong to a new gener-
ation of post-Soviet young writers, whose Soviet memories
chiefly consist of pioneer scarves and holiday camps. It is a
hard place to be: informed, but not defined, by an enemy
that no longer exists; and surrounded by a new generation's
indifference and apathy.

Voltskaia is very much alive to her predicament, and a sense
of estrangement and the perspective of an outsider are key
notes in the collection. Of course, you might argue that being

a melancholic outsider is a standard poetic persona – the
elegiac mode coming very naturally in lyrical poetry. However,
Voltskaia's great strength is that she relates personal
alienation, disappointment in love and solitude, with a sense of
social alienation, alienation from a past, both poetic and
historical, and the alienation of a city, St Petersburg, from the
mainstream of Russian life. The convergence of these strands is
what makes her poetry so rich and many-sided – also, perhaps,
what makes it difficult for the reader who is not within the
context of Russia. Undoubtedly most English language readers
will fasten more readily onto her poems of love and love lost.
Poems such as 'Longbow' which describe the erotic battle of
sex, in which the lyrical voice is a bow, and the lover is
Odysseus, trusting his bow more than Penelope, and then
Apollo, smiling brightly at Niobe, whilst he takes aim at her
children.

Voltskaia makes her inheritance plain. The classicism of her
poems, the formal shape and intimate tone of them stand in a
poetic tradition long associated with St Petersburg. There
are many references to St Petersburg predecessors, but none
as explicit and repeated as those to Joseph Brodsky. In the
poem 'On the possibility of Joseph Brodsky's return' she calls
Brodsky Orpheus, and repeatedly asks him not to come back to
that underworld, St Petersburg, where the inhabitants are
merely 'the shadows of his lines', their clothes no longer 'nice
enough' for him to press his lips against. The anxiety of poetic
succession, the need to 'make contact' with Brodsky, which she
describes in her essay 'On the ruins of our Rome 4', pervade
Voltskaia's work – she makes poetry out of the underworld she
inhabits, paradoxically reanimating Petersburg poetry with
that very material of shadows and corpses.

The issue of poetic succession is far more fraught in Russia
than it is here. This is Auden's centenary year, a poet Brodsky
revered, and yet there aren't many British poets of Voltskaia's
generation queuing up to inherit Auden's mantle. You might
argue this is because of the position the poet traditionally

occupied in Russia. Poetry has long been considered a mystical gift, the poet an oracle, with a moral and almost religious power. But in Voltskaia's essays she describes the current erosion of this power and the changing relationship between reader and poet: 'the poet and the contemporary reader are lovers', the public, in other words, shifts to the intimate. In Voltskaia's work there is a constant search for poetics which bind the grand past to this new private era.

Voltskaia is at her most inspiring for me when she turns her lyrical gifts and sharp sight towards the natural world. Her descriptions of the rain eating into the snow in 'Like a vampire . . .' for example:

> Like a vampire, rain drinks from winter
> Through the holes it's torn in her fine white lace . . .

Or in 'Thaw', where circles have thawed around the pine trees 'as though / around tired eyes . . .' This is a rare attention to natural detail – something I miss when I read contemporary Russian poetry, which is often urban in preoccupation and setting.

Emily Lygo's translations of Voltskaia are exemplary in many ways. She manages to remain as close as possible to the Russian word order, let alone the language and images of the work. Very little is 'smoothed out' to ease the translator's path. At the same time she produces translations which in most cases make the successful transition to English poetry, and even when this is not possible (the original subject matter or style too alien) there are lines and phrases of great beauty and emotional delicacy. She has chosen to rhyme loosely or to use half-rhyme and pararhyme to indicate a Russian classical form. This allows the ghost of the original to appear, without overwhelming the English.

There are problems for the translator of Voltskaia, although Lygo, and Catriona Kelly, whose translations are also included here, generally overcome them. Her language and imagery are

so terribly compressed in Russian that they threaten to sprawl
and unravel endlessly in English. Then there are the problems
of tone. Long poems such as 'Shadow' in which the lyrical
persona is a shadow, oppressed and forced to fit in, her shadowy
nature the result of unhappy love, or 'Little Elegy', in which
the extraordinary and moving description of summer becoming
winter is marred for me by the final line 'Only you're not with
me'. Without the strictness of the Russian shape this tone can
seem a little self-indulgent and mawkish. But it is still the case
that Voltskaia is a complex and inspiring poet, and this
collection a welcome addition to the little Russian poetry we
have in good translation.

Sasha Dugdale

After Every War: Twentieth-Century Women Poets
Translations from the German by Eavan Boland
Princeton University Press
ISBN 0-691-12779-4
Pb 168pp. £8.50

Ingeborg Bachmann / Hans Werner Henze
Briefe einer Freundschaft
Piper Verlag
ISBN 3-492-04608-8
Hb 538pp

This anthology by Eavan Boland is very idiosyncratic, but that
is not meant as a criticism – all anthologies are to a greater or
lesser degree idiosyncratic, and Boland emphasises the personal
nature of this one in her Introduction: when she was a child in
Ireland, two German sisters came to help in the house as a way
of escaping the harsh conditions of post-war Germany. They
gave her an early intimacy with German and, retrospectively,

through that language, a connection to 'the very heart of a broken Europe'. It is as witnesses to the brokenness of twentieth-century Europe that the poets here are presented, their poems being understood as animate and animating reminders of how large-scale events (wars and their after-effects) touch the most hidden and ungraspable parts of our lives, for 'the delicacy and actuality of a place in its time can quickly be overwritten'. Saying this, Boland also has the Troubles in Ireland in mind and the way poetry responded to them, forming a further personal impulse for the book.

What the anthology does offer is selections of widely varying length from the work of Rose Ausländer, Elisabeth Langgässer, Nelly Sachs, Gertrud Kolmar, Else Lasker-Schüler, Ingeborg Bachmann, Marie Luise Kaschnitz, Hilde Domin and Dagmar Nick, in that order, though it corresponds neither to their birth-dates nor to the dates of the poems chosen, nor to anything else that I could discern. That seems to be a conscious attempt, having set out quite a specific historical context in the Introduction, to discourage us from reading the poems historically, and in the same spirit poems are not dated or even presented in chronological order within the selection from each poet. I would have quite liked to have the dates, but I can see why Boland has preferred not to. The dates of birth range from 1869 (Lasker-Schüler) to 1926 (Bachmann and Nick), so the poets come from about three different generations and have not all lived through the same wars. All wrote in German, though they were born throughout the German-speaking parts of Europe, from Czernowitz to Klagenfurt, from Breslau to Cologne (Boland provides helpful maps but seems to think Czernowitz north of Berlin when (now called Chernovtsy) it lies on about the same latitude as Munich), and were scattered much more widely by Hitler. Six out of the nine were Jewish. Only Nick is still alive, though Domin died only last year, after this book first came out in 2004. All have been translated to some extent before, but much here will be unfamiliar to most. The poems appear in the original German (with very frequent misprints) and in Boland's mostly excellent translations. There are also bibliographical lists for each poet, gathering titles in German as well as English.

Two of the most striking things about the poems themselves is how resolutely lyrical they are and how obliquely, if at all, war makes its presence felt in them. Bachmann's poem 'Every Day' begins: 'War is no longer declared: /Just continued. The unheard-of/has become the quotidian'. But even this sense of war being continued by other means, almost a defining principle behind Bachmann's writing, is quite direct within the context of the book, with Kaschnitz's 'Hiroshima' a definite exception. On a couple of occasions Boland includes a note to help us understand the connection better, as with Langgässer's fraught poem 'Spring 1946', written on her daughter's return from Auschwitz, but otherwise she leaves the language of the poems to speak for itself, or in her equivalent of its fragile-but-resilient, fractured-but-healing force. Take Nelly Sachs's 'In This Amethyst':

> Age-old nighttime is
> stored in this amethyst.
> An early intelligence of light
> set fire to this sadness
> which then still flowed,
> still wept.
>
> And still your dying shines –
> hard violet.

A lot of the poems here are as discreet as this amethyst; they read like compacted and distilled glimpses of an unspoken pain that their form both expresses and retains. Boland's translation is characteristically sympathetic and sure-footed, though the imponderables of translation emerge in the last word, whose German original means the flower and only by association the colour. So some of the transformation and vulnerability implied perhaps gets lost or at least subdued. Shelley compared translation itself to throwing a violet into a crucible. Boland certainly makes it seem a good deal more hopeful than that, indeed vital, and one of the best things about this book is that it contains not just nine poets, but ten. Reading it, there is a repeated sense of how what looks like the edge of things is in fact the centre. And in the end there is little to distinguish this anthology from a representative selection of women poets writing in German over the last century (up until the seventies at least), which says a lot about what we did in it. 'I was injured on this earth', Else Lasker-Schüler says in 'Autumn', a poem published in Jerusalem in 1943.

Boland gives Ingeborg Bachmann particular attention, both in the introduction and by the number of pages devoted to her work. Bachmann's correspondence with the composer Hans Werner Henze is the first major one of hers to be published. The two first met at a meeting of the Gruppe 47 in 1952 when they were both 26, and the relationship that grew from there continued in various forms and with varying intensity until Bachmann's death in 1973. Much of the correspondence is in Italian and other languages. There are many more letters from Henze than from Bachmann, partly because he lost some of hers, but it also seems that he wrote more often. This is not the sort of correspondence that allows you to trace much of the writers' lives – very few letters follow on from one another, a lot is left hanging. They deal largely with their work, some of which they did in collaboration. Their support for each other and faith in each other's work is exemplary. Henze's great belief in work and the importance of having the right conditions in which to do it brings home to you the achievement of the poets in the anthology, who held onto and crystallized so much despite the hostility of their times.

Charlie Louth

Vittorio Sereni
The Selected Poetry and Prose
Translated by Peter Robinson and Marcus Perryman
University of Chicago Press
ISBN 0-226-74878-2
Hb, 441pp, £22.50

Luciano Erba
The Greener Meadow: Selected Poems
Translated by Peter Robinson
Princeton University Press
ISBN 0-691-12764-6
Pb, 271 pp $17.95

Peter Robinson returns to England in spring to take up a professorship at the university of Reading. As harbingers to this return – he has been particularly productive of late – we have two editions of his own poetry (*There Are Avenues* and *Ghost Characters* from Brodie and Shoestring Presses respectively) along with the above. Both of these bilingual texts are a delight, the Sereni in particular. Perryman and Robinson's scholarly edition, which has been twenty-five years in the making, includes an introduction (from Robinson), chronology, illustrations, copious notes and a bibliography, all beautifully packaged by Chicago Press at a snip. Both texts offer faithful translations down to punctuation and line breaks, but they never falter as poems, with the same restrained and careful diction found in Robinson's own poetry.

Robinson describes how Vittorio Sereni's (1913–83) imprisonment in North Africa for the last eighteen months of the war excluded him from taking part in the Italian Resistance. The resulting feelings of frustration, guilt and marginality were, he says (citing Fortini): 'an anger without object, beneath the appearance of perplexity and stupefaction'. These are clearly reflected in Sereni's collection *Algerian Diary* but they continue to impact on his later poetry. Yet Robinson also argues that 'Sereni is above all among the great love poets of what it means to be thoroughly alive'. This seems apt, for Sereni is a philosophical poet who teases out life's enduring qualities, providing a subtle perspective on war that reinforces human transience but steers clear of platitudes of war and loss.

Consider these lines from 'Zenna Road' from his first collection *Frontier* which, though pre-war, takes imminent partings as one of its themes:

> But we'll return silent at each approach to shore,
> be no more than a sound,
> you and I, of voluble hours
> or perhaps short thuds of oars
> from disconsolate boats.

Here we have a touching juxtaposition of loss and love of life; personal memories are wistful, dreamlike and intangible as individual sounds merge with time and immediate objects. Indeed, is this a description of a present or a timeless landscape haunted by ghosts of the past? Similarly in the prose piece 'Sicily '43', which describes Italy's defeat, he shows how history may pass but the land remains permanent and easily able to accommodate change: 'its skies already match a different flag, even before it's materially unfurled and hoisted into the wind.' In 'Frontier' there is a lovely fluidity in his description of how boundaries of time and place shift and disorientate. This also appears in 'Birthday': 'you unfold me another age gleaming, / in a windless road', or 'Image': 'Walk upon the whirlpool of years / howled from the river'.

Human Implements, his most substantial volume and a major award winner, spans twenty years to include the period of Italy's post-war reconstruction. The collection is dominated by a feeling of fracture – as the country rebuilds itself we see Sereni struggling to reconstruct affirmative poetic utterances, ironically more available during the war itself. Many of these

poems have a tone of listlessness such as 'In Sleep': 'I don't like
my times, I don't like them. / Italy will slumber with me.' He
seems less certain about himself as a poet, as 'Windows'
ponders: 'Tell me then if you still know / I'm your song
forever'; it's as though his war experiences have made it
difficult for him to engage with ordinary life, placing him on
the margins. However, we do see him still able to experience
moments of low-key everyday pleasure, as in 'Ashes': 'Too
much ash scatters boredom round itself / joy when it's here in
itself is enough.'

His final collection *Variable Star* continues to engage the
reader with its complexity and its powerful poems on the death
of close friends, while his prose provides insights into his
war-time experience, meditations on his own writing and
tributes to fellow writers. Thus by the end of the volume, it is
clear that Perryman and Robinson have done us a great service
in making such a rich selection of Vittorio Sereni's work
available to the English speaking public.

Luciano Erba (b.1922) gained a useful foothold in 1952 by
becoming associated with the Milanese group of poets of which
Sereni was the senior member, but his poetry is very much his
own: he provides an exuberant 'seize the day' experience that
encourages the jaded reader to fall back in love with life. There
is also a clear progression in his work as he moves from a
spontaneous engagement with the immediate world through a
more reflective attempt to recapture that lost spontaneity to his
final expressions of loss in the later poems.

Take the early poem 'The Red Globules':

> The woman constant in memory
> goes rainbowed down her street today
> in the blink of an eye reawakening
> the world's colours and the madness
> snaking through the districts.

Here the woman's image is so powerful that it transforms the
world around it; making everything heightened and idealised
as though seen in Technicolour – suggestions of those
childhood summers where it is always hot. This leads us nicely
on to the childhood poem 'Yellow Orris' with its two young
fishermen: 'They'll reach right to the distant flowers / those
fisherman without good fortune.'

There is something verging on adoration of women of all
shapes and sizes in many poems, all interwoven with numerous
descriptions of clothing, such as in 'Aerostatics': 'your straw
hat / with red ribbons like a gondolier'. In 'La Grande Jeanne'
he transforms a prostitute's words into outpourings of potential
and depth: 'she told me I could save her / and that her world
was there, in my hands.' His euphoria over women is part
of a general argument to live life at full throttle; in 'The
Inattentive' he asks the question: 'if it will return, life /
that's lost through inattention' and in 'Vanitas Varietatum':
'the earth, the earth and every pain of love / does other pain
exist?'

His later poetry shows more awareness of life passing and,
like Sereni, less certainty as in 'Seven and a Half': 'I wouldn't
have known I could understand / and now? I've understood
that I can't know.' 'If This is All' is also darkly humorous: 'I
have obviously understood nothing / will have to think on it
again some more.' Though vivid descriptions of objects still
remain in many of his poems, they are often subordinated to
other issues such as the impending death here in 'Quartiere
Solari':

> my mother knew only too well
> that I wouldn't be a long time near her
> she was smiling nonetheless
> on a background of dahlias and clustered violets.

Taken as a whole Erba's poetry is exuberant, joyful, and full of
respect for what is seen. Robinson argues that he has produced

'one of the most unusual and original bodies of work in contemporary Italian poetry'. It isn't hard to take him at his word; it is wonderful that he has given us a way in.

Belinda Cooke

Shorter Reviews: European Round-Up

Sonja Besford, *memories of summers in brist near gradac and other poems*, Ambit Books, 40pp, paperback, £6.95, ISBN 0-900055-08-1

Sonja Besford's sensual poetry explores her childhood in Serbia, an idyllic time when 'daylights were long, soft, and lazy/ stretching into slow velvety dusks' as the title poem opens. The volume then moves through Lagos in 1973 to the very different Belgrade in the cold winter of 1993/4 where 'pensioners scavenged rubbish containers/for potato-peel' and each 'tired dawn broke/announcing old hungers and many new deaths/ while undertakers sang heavenly songs.' Another excellent publication from Ambit Books.

Richard Burns, *In a Time of Drought*, Shoestring Press, 54pp, paperback, £8.95, ISBN 1-904886-24-8

The poet Richard Burns has long been a champion of Balkan poetry, bringing major poets such as Lalic and Pavlovic to international audiences, especially during his time at the helm of the Cambridge Poetry Festival. It is therefore fitting that, with Shoestring's welcome publication of *In a Time of Drought*, first published in Serbian in 2004 (and for which Burns received the Morava Poetry Prize in 2005), this process is now reversed. An extraordinary book-length poem, based around the Balkan folk tradition of the rain maiden or Dodola, *In a Time of Drought* sees this mythical figure transformed into a symbol of hope and creativity, the healing rain that falls after the storm. Presented in a seven-part sequence, each with seven poems, this is a life-affirming work to 'wash off the stench of war/ Scrub us clean down to our core' (Richard Burns' latest poetry collection *The Blue Butterfly* will be reviewed in the next edition of *MPT*.)

Remco Campert, *I Dreamed in the Cities at Night*, translated by Donald Gardner with an introduction by Paul Vincent, Arc Publications, 138pp, paperback, £9.99, ISBN 978-1904614-36-4

Born in The Hague in 1929, Remco Campert is part of the radical – and influential – group of Dutch poets who came to prominence in the 1950s, although this is his first collection to appear in English. Influenced by jazz, Campert's dry, almost dead-pan voice could be difficult to convey in English but Donald Gardner's versions capture both the lightness and the underlying intensity of the originals: 'Doors are open,' as 'House in Antwerp' wryly observes, 'that will never close again.'

Goethe, *Love As Landscape Painter*, translated by D.M. Black, FRAS Publications, 76pp, paperback, £8.50, ISBN 0-9549941-4-0

Heinrich Heine, *Germany: A Winter's Tale*, translated with introduction and notes by John Goodby, Smokestack Books, 116pp, paperback, £7.99 ISBN 0-9548691-3-3

Two giants of German literature are here reimagined in new translations from two small publishing houses: D. M. Black brings a tautness and elegance to Goethe's classically-influenced work while John Goodby captures Heine's satirical wit with verve.

Marilyn Hacker, *Essays on Departure: New and Selected Poems 1980–2005*, Oxford Poets/Carcanet, 180pp, paperback, £12.95, ISBN 1-903039-78-9

One of North America's most influential poets, Marilyn Hacker has long intermingled classical European forms with contemporary themes in her verse. This excellent introduction to her work from Oxford Poets also contains a selection of her acclaimed translations from Claire Malroux, Guy Goffette and Emmanuel Moses, among others. 'Something unknown melts beneath our footsteps,' as Hacker translates Moses' incandescent poem 'Royal Blue', '. . . but the history which prevails,/is that of churches' white roses'. Essential reading.

Joan Margarit, *Tugs in the Fog: Selected Poems*, translated by Anna Crowe, Bloodaxe Books, 176pp, paperback, £9.95, ISBN 1-85224-751-7

With a well-deserved Poetry Book Society Recommendation, Anna Crowe's excellent translation offers a selection of the Barcelona-based poet's work for English readers. Influenced by Hardy and Larkin, Margarit's intensely moving poems are inhabited by ghosts of the dead: the generation lost in the Spanish Civil War or the generation of poets killed in the First World War, Margarit's parents, his little sister who died of meningitis and most memorably his beloved handicapped daughter Joana who died in 2001. Like the *Odyssey,* employed as a reference point throughout Margarit's work, they trace our journeys in and out of the Underworld with compassion and humanity, as the dead bequeath the living their 'chance for life': 'I stopped' as Crowe translates 'June night' from Margarit's 2002 collection *Ioana*, 'feeling that you were nearby. Feeling that now, / at any moment, I could make death's/ treasures appear.' This compelling volume cannot be recommended too highly.

Paul Merchant, *Some Business of Affinity:* Five Seasons Press, 272pp, hardback, £13.50, ISBN 978-0947960-39-1

Subtitled 'Translations, Reworkings, Interpretations and Responses', *Some Business of Affinity* represents a cross-section of Paul Merchant's work as a poet and translator, including versions of Aeschylus, Catullus, Horace, Dafydd ap Gwilym, as well as Yannis Ritsos (in 1968 *MPT* 4 was devoted to Merchant's translations of twentieth-century Greek poetry). The volume also includes fascinating sequences of what

Merchant terms 'recoveries', here poems based on entries in Coleridge's notebooks. Merchant's interest in the relationship between visual art and the written word – other forms of translation – is evidenced in his sequence of poems inspired by Hokusai, each accompanied by its originating image. In the sequence, 'Crossing Over with A Burden (On Translation)', Merchant explores this relationship even more directly in a powerful exchange of text and image with Oregon artist Steve Tilden. This is a beautifully-produced volume, with over 40 illustrations in all, from the ever-reliable Five Seasons Press – a must-buy for all those interested in translation, poetry or art and, in particular, the intriguing crossroads where all three meet; where 'to draw is to draw together'.

Six Slovenian Poets, edited by Brane Mozetič, Arc Publications, 172pp, paperback, £10.99, ISBN 1-904614-17-5

This is the first in a new series of bilingual anthologies from Arc, with the admirable aim of bringing the work of a younger generation of poets across Europe to a wider English-language readership. *Six Slovenian Poets* fulfils this endeavour with a varied selection of poets under forty, all published for the first time within the past decade and all, in their various ways, breaking with Slovenian literary tradition. These young poets reference the Beckhams, Dolce & Gabbana, Sinéad O'Connor and Gilbert and George as well as Paz, Yeats and Auden: poems, as Gregor Podlogar comments in Ana Jelinkar and Stephen Watts' fine translation, for when '54 TV programmes/ just aren't enough'.

Daniel Weissbort and Astradur Eysteinsson (editors)
Translation – Theory and Practice: A Historical Reader, Oxford University Press, 649pp, hardback, £65, ISBN 0-19-871199-9/paperback, £25 ISBN 0-19-871200-6

Weissbort and Eysteinsson's impressive new volume covers every aspect of translation from the Ancient World to the present day, from the story of Babel in Genesis to Seamus

Heaney's recent version of *Beowulf*, taking in Luther, Dryden, Aphra Benn, Pope, Johnson, Goethe, Longfellow and Browning on the way. At least half the book is devoted to the pioneering work of twentieth-century practitioners and theorists in the field – Pound, Benjamin, Jakobson, Nida, Lowell, Steiner, Bassnett, Venuti – presenting a comprehensive work of reference for translation students, academics and practitioners alike. Clearly a labour of love as well as of erudition, *Translation – Theory and Practice*, promises to become an indispensable text book for the twenty-first century.

Josephine Balmer

Halbe Sachen, edited by Olaf Kutzmutz and Adrian La Salvia, Bundesakademie für kulturelle Bildung, 504pp., paperback, ISBN 978-3-929622-24-9.

The proceedings of colloquia and workshops on translation held in Wolfenbüttel and Erlangen 2004–2006. Mixing theory and practice, the language is German and the focus is on poetry, with translations of Spenser, Yeats, Beckett, H.D., Jeremy Prynne and Vladimír Holan among others, essays on Melville, Rilke, Tsvetaeva, Sartre, Celan, Larkin, a one-acter by Ionesco done into German from the Rumanian, an interview with Georges-Arthur Goldschmidt about translation and Freud, and much else besides. This is a rich and interesting collection.

Charlie Louth

Books for review should be sent to Josephine Balmer, Reviews Editor, *Modern Poetry in Translation*, East Meon, St John's Road, Crowborough, East Sussex, TN6 1RW. The theme for the next round-up will be classic texts.

Notes on Contributors

Timothy Adès is working on a large volume of Robert Desnos, and a second volume of Jean Cassou.

Paul Batchelor's poems have appeared in *MPT*, *The North*, *Poetry London* and *Poetry Review*. In 2003 he was given an Eric Gregory Award. He is writing a PhD on Barry MacSweeney. His pamphlet *To Photograph a Snow Crystal* was recently published by Smith Doorstop.

Peter Clark is an consultant and writer. He has translated extensively from Arabic – novels, history, drama and short stories, and has written books on Henry Hallam, Marmaduke Pickthall and Wilfred Thesiger. He spent 30 years with the British Council, mostly in the Arab world.

Robert Chandler's translations include Pushkin's *Dubrovsky*, Leskov's *Lady Macbeth of Mtsensk*, Vasily Grossman's *Life and Fate* and Hamid Ismailov's *The Railway*, as well as selections of Sappho and Apollinaire. His co-translations of Andrey Platonov have won prizes in the UK and the US. He is the editor of *Russian Short Stories from Pushkin to Buida*.

Belinda Cooke's poetry, reviews and Russian translations have been published widely. She is currently completing an edition of *The Selected Poems of Marina Tsvetaeva*. She lives in Aberdeenshire.

Sasha Dugdale is a consultant and translator for the Royal Court Theatre. Her first collection, *Notebook*, was published in 2003, her second, *The Estate*, in 2007 (both Carcanet Oxford

Poets). Bloodaxe published her translation of Tatiana Shcherbina's *Life Without* in 2004, and they will publish her translation of Elena Shvarts' *Birdsong on the Seabed* early in 2008.

Jonathan Dunne studied Classics at Oxford University and Spanish and Galician at Barcelona and Santiago de Compostela Universities. He translates Manuel Rivas for Harvill in the UK and Overlook in the US, as well as the Spanish author Enrique Vila-Matas and the Catalan author Carme Riera. He is currently working on the translation of contemporary Bulgarian poets.

Robin Fulton's recent publications include a special issue of *Poetry Scotland* (No.26), a revised edition of Robert Garioch's *Collected Poems* (Birlinn), translations of Tranströmer (Bloodaxe and New Directions), O H Hauge (Anvil), and of groups of poems in Chinese, German, Hebrew, Spanish and Swedish.

Marilyn Hacker has published a dozen collections of poems, including *Desesperanto* (Norton, 2003) and *Essays in Departure, New and Selected Poems* (Carcanet/Oxford Poets 2006). She is the translator of, among other titles, Vénus Khoury-Gata's *She Says* (Graywolf, 2003) and Claire Malroux's *Birds and Bison* (Sheep Meadow, 2004).

Michael Hamburger's *Circling the Square,* a new collection of poems, and the third edition of his *Poems of Paul Celan,* have just been published by Anvil Press.

Paul Harris studied Chinese poetry at Oxford in the 1960s under David Hawkes. He was then for over thirty years a translator in the financial sector. Now retired, he has the time to pursue his more humane interests and enjoy the opportunities of travel to China that hardly existed in the 1960s.

Mark Leech's most recent book of translations, *Anglo Saxon Voices*, is published by Pipers' Ash Ltd. He won the Stephen Spender prize for poetry in translation in 2004, and has had poems and translations published in a wide range of magazines. He lives in Oxford

Charlie Louth teaches German at Queen's College, Oxford. He is the author of *Hölderlin and the Dynamics of Translation*. He has also translated Hölderlin's letters and is now at work on a critical introduction to Rilke.

Sarah Maguire is the founder and director of the Poetry Translation Centre at SOAS. Her fourth collection of poems, *The Pomegranates of Kandahar*, will be published by Chatto & Windus in June, 2007. With Yama Yari, she co-translated the novel *A Thousand Rooms of Dream and Fear*, by the Afghan writer, Atiq Rahimi (Chatto & Windus, 2006). She is currently co-translating the leading Sudanese poet, Al-Saddiq Al-Raddi.

Paul Merchant was the editor/translator of *MPT* 4 (1968). His poetry collections are *Stones* (1973), *Salt Water Island* (1983), *Bone from a Stag's Heart* (1988 Poetry Book Society Recommendation), and *Some Business of Affinity* (2006). Since 1996 he has been Director of the William Stafford Archives in Oregon.

Stephanie Norgate's poems have appeared in *Oxford Poets 2000* , *Forward Poems of the Decade, Magma, Poetry London, The Poetry Cure* (Bloodaxe 2005), *Reactions 3, MsLexia* and elsewhere. Bloodaxe will publish a volume of her poetry, *Hidden River,* next year. Her five-part dramatisation of Elizabeth L. Banks *The Journalistic Adventures of An American Girl in London* was the Woman Hour's Serial on Radio 4 in 2003.

J.P. Nosbaum's most recent publications include poems in *Poetry Review* and *MPT*. Originally from the US, he has spent the last dozen years in Britain and currently lives in Bedford.

The Norwich Zanzotto project (described more fully in *In Other Words* 28) came about under the aegis of poet and translator Peter Waterhouse – instigator of the 9-volume collaborative German Zanzotto project *Planet Beltà* – during his Leverhulme Visiting Professsorship at the University of East Anglia in 2006. His latest prose work, 2006, is *(Krieg und Welt)*. Will Buck, Megan Clark, Jonathan Evans, and Stefan Tobler took the MA in Literary Translation at UEA in 2005/6. Aaron Deveson and Eugenia Loffredo are currently Associate Tutors in Literature at UEA, where Jo Catling also lectures in German and Comparative Literature. She has published on Rilke and other German-language authors e.g. W. G. Sebald.

Oliver Reynolds is an usher at the Royal Opera House. His last book of poems was *Almost* (1999).

Stephen Romer's fourth collection, *Yellow Studio*, is due from Carcanet's OxfordPoet's series in early 2008. He edited Faber's *20th-century French Poems* (2002) and is currently working on an anthology of younger French poets in translation. His selected poems in French translation, *Tribut*, appeared in February 2007, from Editions Le temps qu'il fait.

Mike Stocks' novel *White Man Falling* – winner of the 2006 Goss First Novel Award – and his collection of sonnets *Folly* are published by Alma Books. His book of Giuseppe Belli translations *Sonnets* is published by Oneworld Classics in June 2007. He is the editor of the poetry magazine *Anon.* His website is www.mikestocks.com.

Cristina Viti's version of Eros Alesi's *Fragments* appeared in *MPT* 3/3. Her current work includes some lyrics for the forthcoming album of the Milanese music project Mordecai and an Italian translation of the poetry of Stephen Watts.

Andrew Wachtel is Professor of the Humanities at Northwestern University and a member of the American Academy of Arts and Sciences. He is the author of ten books and more than a hundred articles on Russian and South Slavic literature, culture, and society. In 2004 he published Anzhelina Polonskaya, *A Voice. Selected Poems* (Northwestern University Press).

MODERN POETRY IN TRANSLATION   Series 3   Number 1

INTRODUCTIONS

Edited by David and Helen Constantine
Cover by Chris Hyde

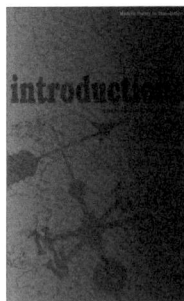

Contents

Editorial   David and Helen Constantine

Mahmoud Darwish *A State of Siege*, translated by Sarah Maguire and Sabry Hafez

Boris Ryzhy, nine poems, translated by Sasha Dugdale

Giorgio Caproni, *Ligurian Suite*, translated by Robert Hahn

Liam Ó Muirthile, five poems, translated by Bernard O'Donoghue

Eunice Odio, 'Ode to the Hudson', translated by Keith Ekiss and Mauricio Espinoza

Luciano Erba, eleven poems, translated by Peter Robinson

Philippe Jaccottet, from *Green Notebook*, translated by Helen and David Constantine

Jorge Yglesias, Two short essays and five poems, translated by Peter Bush

Gerhard Falkner, seven poems, translated by Richard Dove

'The Traveller' – *A Tribute to Michael Hamburger*, by Charlie Louth

Price £11
Available from www.mptmagazine.com

MODERN POETRY IN TRANSLATION   Series 3   Number 2

DIASPORA

Edited by David and Helen Constantine
Cover by Lucy Wilkinson

Contents
Editorial   David and Helen Constantine

Carmen Bugan, an essay and two poems
Yannis Ritsos, fifteen *Tristichs,* translated by David Harsent
David Harsent, three poems from *Legion*
Goran Simic, an essay and four prose poems
Forough Farrokhzad, four poems, translated by Gholamreza Sami Gorgan Roodi
Marzanna Bogumila Kielar, six poems, translated by Elzbieta Wójcik-Leese
Lyubomor Nikolov, six poems, introduced by Clive Wilmer, translated Miroslav Nikolov
Adel Guémar, four poems, translated by Tom Cheesman and John Goodby
A note on Hafan Books by Tom Cheesman
Sándor Márai, 'Funeral Oration', translated by George Gömöri and Clive Wilmer
Paul Batchelor, versions of Ovid's *Tristia*
Olivia McCannon, three poems
Yvonne Green, three poems
Ziba Karbassi, three poems, translated by Stephen Watts
Volker Braun, nine poems, translated by David Constantine
Wulf Kirsten, ten poems, translated by Stefan Tobler
Knut Ødegaard 'Taking out the Hives' translated by Kenneth Steven
Eugenio Montale, three uncollected poems, translated by Simon Carnell and Erica Segre

Reviews
Bernard Adams on George Szirtes's Agnes Nemes Nagy
Paschalis Nicolaou on David Connolly's Yannis Kondos
Will Stone on Antony Hasler's Georg Heym

Price £11
Available from www.mptmagazine.com

MODERN POETRY IN TRANSLATION   Series 3   Number 3

METAMORPHOSES

Edited by David and Helen Constantine
Cover by Lucy Wilkinson

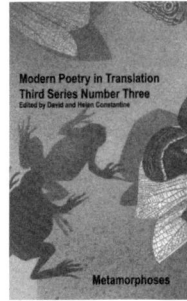

Contents

Editorial   David and Helen Constantine

Akhmatova on the South Bank
Ruth Borthwick: Anna of all the Russias: Translating Akhmatova
Elaine Feinstein: An Evening for Akhmatova
Colette Bryce: Six poems
Sasha Dugdale: Five poems
Jo Shapcott: Five poems
George Szirtes (with Veronika Krasnova): Six poems
Marilyn Hacker: 'For Anna Akhmatova'

John Greening: 'Coming Soon. *Remastered from the Old Norse*'
Neil Philip: 'Twenty-one glosses on poems from *The Greek Anthology*'
Paul Howard: Versions of four sonnets by Giuseppe Belli
Terence Dooley: A version of Raymond Queneau's 'La Pendule'
Kathleen Jamie: Hölderlin into Scots. Two poems
Josephine Balmer: *The Word for Sorrow:* a work begins its progress

Ingeborg Bachmann
Karen Leeder: Introduction
Mike Lyons: 'War Diary'
Patrick Drysdale and Mike Lyons: Five poems

Sean O'Brien: A version of Canto V of Dante's *Inferno*
Cristina Viti: Eros Alesi's *Fragments*
Sarah Lawson and Malgorzata Koraszweska: Six poems by Anna
Kühn-Cichocka
Marilyn Hacker: Guy Goffette's 'Construction-Site of the Elegy'
Belinda Cooke and Richard McCane: Six poems by Boris Poplavsky
Cecilia Rossi: Poems from Alejandra Pizarnik's *Works and Nights*
Terence Cave: A memorial note on Edith McMorran and a transla-
tion of Aragon's 'C'
Paul Batchelor: An essay on Barry MacSweeney's Apollinaire

Reviews

Antony Wood on Angela Livingstone's *Poems from Chevengur*
Josephine Balmer on Cliff Ashcroft's *Dreaming of Still Water* and
Peter Boyle's Eugenio Montejo
Paschalis Nikolaou on Philip Ramp's Karouzos
Francis Jones on Jan Twardowski (translated by Sarah Lawson and
Malgorzata Koraszweska) and *A Fine Line: New Poetry from Central
and Eastern Europe*

Price £11
Available from www.mptmagazine.com

MODERN POETRY IN TRANSLATION   Series 3   Number 4

BETWEEN THE LANGUAGES

Edited by David and Helen Constantine

Cover by Lucy Wilkinson

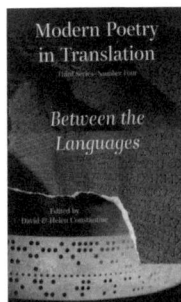

Contents

Editorial   David and Helen Constantine

Kapka Kassabova Polyglot Peregrinations
Amarjit Chandan Inhabiting two Planets
Itsik Manger Four Poems, with translations and a literal version, introduced by Helen Beer
Michael Hamburger Afterthoughts on the Mug's Game
Mary-Ann Constantine To let in the light: Gwyneth Lewis's Poetry of Transition.
Gwyneth Lewis Two Poems, translated by Mary-Ann Constantine and the author
Choman Hardi Switching Languages: a Hindrance or an Opportunity?
Poet to Poet The Scotland-China Project. Introduction by Polly Clark
Antonella Anedda Five Poems, translated by Jamie McKendrick
Dimitris Tsaloumas Four Poems, translated, with an introduction, by Helen Constantine

Extracts from **Mourid Barghouti**'s *Midnight*, translated by Radwa Ashour
'Dear Fahimeh', translated by Hubert Moore and Nasrin Parvaz
Extracts from **Sherko Berkes's** *The Valley of Butterfly*, translated by Choman Hardi
Ingeborg Bachmann Ten Poems, translated by Patrick Drysdale and Mike Lyons, with an introduction by Karen Leeder
Rimbaud Versions of Three Poems, by Martin Bennett
Bertolt Brecht Ten Poems of Exile, translated by Timothy Adès
Ivan Radoev Three Poems, translated by Kapka Kassabova

Anthony Rudolf Any Ideas? Calling all Poetry Detectives

Josephine Balmer A Note on Reviewing Translation

Reviews

Olivier Burckhardt on Claire Malroux's *Birds and Bison*, translated by Marilyn Hacker

Sasha Dugdale on Ileana Mălăncioiu's, *After the Raising of Lazarus,* translated by Eiléan Ní Chuilleanáin

Price £11
Available from www.mptmagazine.com

MODERN POETRY IN TRANSLATION   Series 3   Number 5

TRANSGRESSIONS

Edited by David and Helen Constantine

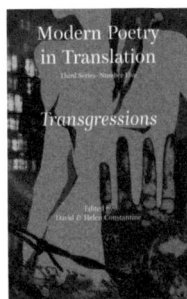

Cover by Lucy Wilkinson

Contents

Editorial   David and Helen Constantine

Four Mansi songs, translated by Dorothea Grünzweig and Derk Wynand
Meles Negusse, 'Wild Animals', translated by Charles Cantalupo and Ghirmai Negash
Hubert Moore, 'Removals'
Sasha Dugdale, 'Lot's Wife'
Pascale Petit, three poems and a translation of a poem by Zhou Zan
Andreas Angelakis, 'Constantine in Constantinople', translated by John Lucas
Constantine Cavafy, two poems, translated into Scots, via the French, by John Manson
Victor Manuel Mendiola, 'Your Hand, My Mouth' translated by Ruth Fainlight
An extract from **Bernard O'Donoghue's** translation of *Sir Gawain*
W.D. Jackson, two versions of Boccaccio
Helen Constantine, Banned Poems

Jean Follain, seven poems, translated by Olivia McCannon
Doris Kareva, three poems, translated by Ilmar Lehtpere
Hilda Domin, 'To whom it happens', translated by Ruth Ingram
Lyubomir Nikolov, three poems, translated by Clive Wilmer and Viara Tcholakova
Rilke, four poems from the *Book of Hours*, translated by Susan Ranson
Amina Saïd, four poems, translated by Marilyn Hacker
Jeff Nosbaum, versions from the *Aeneid* and the *Iliad*
Hsieh Ling-yün, 'By the Stream', translated by Alastair Thomson via the Spanish of Octavio Paz
Yu Xuanji, two poems, translated by Justin Hill
Kaneko Misuzu, four poems, translated by Quentin Crisp

Günter Grass, 'The Ballerina', translated by Michael Hamburger

Robert Hull, One Good Translation Deserves Another

Reviews
Olivia McCannon on Peter Dale's Tristan Corbière
Timothy Adès on Colin Sydenham's Horace
Paschalis Nikolaou on Richard Burns
Belinda Cooke on *Sailor's Home: A Miscellany of Poetry*, and Piotr Sommer's *Continued.*

Shorter Reviews and Further Books Received

Price £11
Available from www.mptmagazine.com

MODERN POETRY IN TRANSLATION   Series 3   Number 6

AFTER-IMAGES

Edited by David and Helen Constantine

Cover by Lucy Wilkinson

Contents
Editorial   David and Helen Constantine

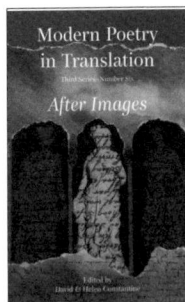

Brecht on the South Bank
Translations and Poems 'after Brecht' by Adrian Mitchell, Andy Croft, Lavinia Greenlaw, Ulrike Draesner, Iain Galbraith, David Constantine, Bert Papenfuss, Andrew Duncan, Albert Ostermaier and Tom Cheesman – introduced by Karen Leeder

Bertolt Brecht, four new Herr Keuner Stories and a short Reflection on the Constitution, translated by Tom Kuhn
Gonçalo Tavares, five stories, translated by Desirée Jung
Thomas Brasch, five poems, translated by Ken Cockburn
Mimi Khalvati, five ghazals
Damian Walford Davies, 'Kilvert', with illustrations by Lucy Wilkinson
Ellen Coverdale, two poems after Lorenzetti and Courbet
Pascale Petit, two poems after René Magritte and Leonor Fini
Jeff Nosbaum, 'Ukiyo-e', after Ryoi
Alison Brackenbury, '1.15 a.m.'
Tara Bergin, 'Himalayan Balsam for a Soldier', after Christina Rossetti's 'Winter: My Secret'
Oliver Reynolds, 'MVM'
David Hart, 'He came mute . . .'
Andrea Zanzotto, 'Hypersonnet', translated by Peter Hainsworth
Tom Cheesman, 'Owain Glyndŵr Explained to an Algerian Asylum-Seeker – Act V'
Robert Hull, two poems
R. Cheran, 'I could forget all this . . .', translated by Lakshmi Holmström

Waldo Williams, 'The Dead Children', translated by Damian Walford Davies
Mario Luzi, two poems, translated by Elizabeth MacDonald
Dorothea Grünzweig, three poems, translated by Derk Wynand
Vyacheslav Kupriyanov, four poems, translated by Dasha Nisula

Poems from Aldeburgh
Naomi Jaffa, Poets and their Translators at Aldeburgh
Joan Margarit, six poems, translated by Anne Crowe
Durs Grünbein, three poems, translated by Michael Hofmann

Peter France, In Memory of Gennady Aygi: Translation and Community
Francis Jones, Stroking Hands over the Heart

Reviews
Anna Reckin on Yang Lian and Zeng Danyi
Belinda Cooke on Clive Scott and Ruth Fainlight
Josephine Balmer, Short Reviews and Further Books Received

Price £11
Available from www.mptmagazine.com

MPT Subscription Form

<table>
<tr><td>Name

Phone
E-mail</td><td>Address

Postcode
Country</td></tr>
</table>

I would like to subscribe to *Modern Poetry in Translation* (please tick relevant box):

Subscription Rates (including postage by surface mail)

	UK	Overseas
❏ One year subscription (2 issues)	£22	£26 / US$ 48
❏ Two year subscription (4 issues) with discount	£40	£48 / US$ 88

Student Discount*

	UK	Overseas
❏ One year subscription (2 issues)	£16	£20 / US$ 37
❏ Two year subscription (4 issues)	£28	£36 / US$ 66

Please indicate which year you expect to complete your studies 20 . . .

Standing Order Discount (only available to UK subscribers)
❏ Annual subscription (2 issues)   £20
❏ Student rate for annual subscription (2 issues)*   £14

Payment Method (please tick appropriate box)

❏ **Cheque:** please make cheques payable to: *Modern Poetry in Translation.*
Sterling, US Dollar and Euro cheques accepted.

❏ **Standing Order:** please complete the standing order request below, indicating the date you would like your first payment to be taken. This should be at least one month after you return this form. We will set this up directly with your bank. Subsequent annual payments will be taken on the same date each year. For UK only.

<table>
<tr><td>Bank Name
Branch Address

Post Code
Sort Code
Account Number</td><td>Account Name
❏ Please notify my bank
Please take my first payment on
......./......./......... and future payments on
the same date each year.
Signature:
Date........./......./............</td></tr>
</table>

Bank Use Only: In favour of Modern Poetry in Translation, Lloyds TSB, 1 High St, Carfax, Oxford, OX1 4AA, UK a/c 03115155 Sort-code 30-96-35

Please return this form to: The Administrator, Modern Poetry in Translation, The Queen's College, Oxford, OX1 4AW   administrator@mptmagazine/www.mptmagazine.com